SOUTHERN WAY

Special Issue No 5

CW00548667

WARTIME SOUTHER[N]

© Kevin Robertson (Noodle Books) and then various contributors 2010

ISBN 978-1-906419-37-0

First published in 2010 by Kevin Robertson
under the **NOODLE BOOKS** imprint
PO Box 279
Corhampton
SOUTHAMPTON
SO32 3ZX
www.kevinrobertsonbooks.co.uk

Printed in England by
The Information Press
Eynsham

PREPARATIONS
FOR ATTACK

We start our trawl through the archives the year before war was declared, 1938, but a time when the deteriorating situation in Europe made conflict appear ever more likely - except that is to certain politicians hopefully waving pieces of paper!

On a more serious note, already the railway was gearing up towards the necessary preparations, as witness here. Not, I must admit, even on the SR, but a scene no doubt repeated on all four of the railway companies.

It is of course Gas Mask training, the location several hundred miles north of the SR, at Blackpool.

The image is from the Corbis Press Agency, whether it was ever actually used at the time is open to doubt. Indeed its very portrayal could well be taken to both encourage or reduce morale, dependent upon the individual viewpoint.

No excuse for its inclusion though, I promise it is also the only non-SR view in this volume, but who resist the scene of a group of railwayman in such pose?

Corbis Images HU048497

Holiday crowds at Waterloo?

At first glimpse perhaps yes, but look more carefully and the number of service personnel present presents the clue. Even more noticeable are the number of individuals sporting gas masks. We have no date,* the smiling soldier is no clue, although clearly the presence of the photographer has aroused more than a little interest from the throng. (Notice too the fashion trend of the time: there appears to be only one male who it hat-less).

Seeing a group such as this, one is immediately reminded of the terrible consequences that could result from air attack at such a time, as indeed did take place, not just of course at Waterloo. The presence of the bus in the background could well be a clue, the evacuation of children thus immediately comes to mind although none appear present.

* almost certainly early in the conflict - up to the end of 1941. By that time, the forage cap and service cap had given way to the beret.

Introduction

I had absolutely no idea the amount of interest there would be in the first volume of this series and it is then with great pleasure that I humbly submit Part 2 for your perusal.

At the time of the release of the first book, in April 2009, I have to admit I was quietly hopeful it might strike a chord, I think the illustrations alone did that, hence I am as grateful as ever to those individuals and organisations it is a pleasure to record below.

As before I do not attempt to set out a full detailed history of those difficult years, instead a photographic record of various locations, incidents and events, taking this time a slightly wider concept than the standard topic, 'Enemy Action'. Even so a number of the latter are still included, although as before I will be the first to admit there are still gaps.

On the last page of this book I make reference to a possible third book in this Wartime Southern series. That is a distinct possibility, although as I write this I should add it is currently an idea for the future and will depend on slightly more material being uncovered. Please then, (the usual plea), I would like to produce it but to do so will need YOUR help. (At this stage the finger of Kitchener in the renowned WW1 poster comes to mind, "Your publisher needs you!)

Returning to the topic in question and as one born post-war, I find I am humbled reading the stories of those who endured so much. The renowned names and locations of conflict are known, herein it is a pleasure to record some of the stories of the lesser known but who each played a valuable role.

Whilst this project has by its very concept to be considered commercially viable, it is still a privilege to present the following pages as a tribute to those times.

Kevin Robertson

ACKNOWLEDGEMENTS and BIBLIOGRAPHY

The compilation of the first book in the *Southern Way Wartime Series* came about as a result of a chance conversation with Stephen Duffell in September 2008, as indeed has been recounted previously.

This second book again draws heavily on the archives of the Railway, Canal & Historical Society and in addition a source made available to us since the release of the first book. This new collection is held by Jeremy Cobb, the grandson of Allan Cobb. Mr Cobb (Senior), commenced his career as a Premium Apprentice at Ashford in 1900, subsequently rising through the ranks on the Motive Power (Operating) Department of the SECR and SR. Although we cannot be certain, the photographs contained within his archive may well relate to incidents he attended during his career. (An article on Mr Cobb - Senior, is in preparation for a forthcoming issue of 'The Southern Way').

Mention and thanks are also due to a new friend, John Atkinson, who has kindly provided much detail relative to stock damaged at this time. John's records appear in this work. Also to Alastair Wilson for bringing to my attention and then transcribing the wonderfully contemporary Junction 'X'.

Again and as before, 'War on the Line' by Bernard Darwin (reprinted by Middleton Press) and, more recently, 'London Main Line War Damage', by B W L Brooksbank (Capital Transport), have proven invaluable.

Other sources, other than those referred to in the text include, 'Southampton's Railways' by Bert Moody - Kingfisher / Atlantic: 'The Elham Valley Line' by Brian Hart - Wild Swan, and various issues of the 'Southern Railway Magazine'

Front cover - 22 March 1946, the only image in this book that is post-war although the presence of service personnel on the train may well mean these were men on their way to being de-mobbed. The mobile tea trolley is of passing interest: built at the Lancing, it enabled hot drinks to be served directly to passengers - one may wonder exactly how many cups were lost in this fashion. The design is very much of its time. *Corbis Images HU024202*

Rear cover - Between 1941 and 1944, two 12 inch mobile guns were stabled on the former Elham Valley line in Kent. Officially referred to as 'Boche-Buster' weapons these huge machines were only able to be fired when the barrel was parallel with the track. Other Southern lines in the area Dover / Folkestone area were used in similar fashion, although as seen here, when fired at right-angles, some degree of anchorage was also required.

Corbis Images HU060968

ON THE HOME FRONT

Consequent upon the declaration of hostilities on 3 September 1939, the priorities for the railway changed overnight. True, up to that time some preparations had been made, but there was still the general hope amongst the nation that somehow we might be able to pull back from the brink. As is well known that was not the case, and thus from 11.00 on that fateful day the railway changed from one where the priority had been service to passengers and freight customers, to one where it was now a vital artery in the movement of men, machinery and supplies to enable the enemy to be fought: as well as well providing transport for materials necessary in this task.

During the following five and a half years there was hardly a single route or type of service that was not affected by delay or disruption, whilst behind the scenes work continued not just on normal scheduled maintenance, but to effect necessary, initially temporary, repairs, to both restore and keep traffic flowing. It has been said many times before, but is relevant to repeat here, what half a century later we take a week or more to carry out was accomplished in a single day, without the multitude of managers, inspectors and forms to complete. One might think then the workforce were vulnerable and exposed to danger, but the statistics do not back up any more injuries to staff occurring as a result.

Left - *Evacuation at a Southern terminal at London, (possibly Waterloo), in June 1940. Mass evacuation of children and other vulnerable individuals had taken place in late August / early September 1939 (see the first volume in this series), but with the feared air-attacks not arriving and Britain entering what would later become known as the 'phoney war' period, many families had their children returned to them. The start of the bombing of London changed all that, although the true 'Blitz' did not begin until September 1940. These evacuees are seen entraining with the assistance of a Guard and WPCs from the Metropolitan Police. Both views were no doubt intended as morale boosting images.*

Corbis Images HU036112 and HU036114

Above - *One view that would certainly not have passed the censor was that above. A German liveried freight wagon at Dover in January 1945 and where it had lain since 1939. The camouflage on the neighbouring building will be noted. All of these had arrived in England via the peacetime train-ferry service and were then impounded and used for storage. The chimneys alone would render them out-of-gauge. January 1945.*

The underground air-raid shelter at Waterloo utilised the vacant space under the various arches. This facility was ruled over by Mr Greenfield, who doubled as the Waterloo Station Master and also Chief Warden. 6,500 people could be accommodated and during particularly heavy raids it would be filled to capacity. 500 of these spaces were permanently taken by bombed-out families, provided with bunks, who brought with them what odd items they might have been able to salvage. The shelters were finally closed on 7 May 1945. (Another portion of the area underneath Waterloo contained a separate shelter for Headquarters Office Staff but with tables, chairs and telephones to enable work to continue during a raid. A further segregated area housed even more telephones and was intended as the emergency control office should an invader approach too close to Deepdene itself - see page 81.)

" GROW GREENS FOR GUYS ! "

The "Dig for Victory" movement has provided quite a harvest for patients in Guys Hospital.

"By kind permission of the Directors of the Southern Railway" (as states *Guys Hospital Gazette*) "and with the willing co-operation of the London Bridge Station", travellers were invited by a notice at London Bridge Station to deposit the surplus produce of their garden or allotment on a table in the Station for the patients of Guys. The scheme was organised by the Guild of ex-Patients and the offerings were collected daily by the nurses. The collection was open from September 7th to October 3rd, and in those 23 days the number of small parcels of vegetables and fruit helped substantially to feed Guys' many patients. Most numerous gifts were of apples (369 pounds), while there were 237 cabbages and 100 marrows. Beans, beetroots, blackberries, carrots, cauliflowers, celery, cucumbers—the offerings went right through the alphabet down to watercress, of which there were no less than 89 bundles, while the contributions showed welcome variety—there were even three pounds of figs, five nectarines and nine pumpkins !

Next year the organiser (Mr. Sidney, Hon. Sec. of the Guild of ex-Patients) hopes that, with the Company's permission, he will be able to make an earlier start to the scheme.

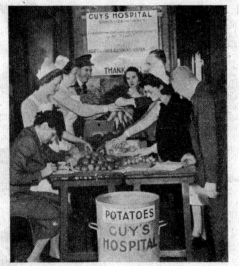

Gathering the harvest for Guy's.

Air raid shelter alongside the line at East Worthing with a number of allotments alongside. Between 1939 and 1945, the Brighton area, which included Worthing, was the subject of some 1,010 'Red' warnings (- meaning enemy overhead), all but one of these in the years 1940 - 1944.

The allotments alongside were another feature of the period, the Southern Railway releasing land so that by 1943 there were a total of 13,000 separate plots covering some 600 acres.

As a means of encouraging such enterprise, regular allotment shows were also held throughout the system.

West Sussex Museum Service PP/WSL/WGP001645

Waterloo, 'sometime between 1939 and 1945'.

"We of the travelling public always have a good many questions to ask and if our own are of course 'really necessary' those of other people seem sometimes superfluous, especially now that the unseen announcer, apparently in the roof, tells us so much by loudspeaker. It is a matter in which we are acutely conscious of one another's little weaknesses. In war time, however, there inevitably arose a number of questions that really did need asking and answering. Especially in the time of air raids - the problem of alternative routes was a constant one. Soldiers fresh from overseas naturally wanted to know how to get to their homes. So during the blitz in 1940 the giving of advice to travellers was systematically organised, primarily to help travellers when lines were blocked by bomb damage. Enquiry kiosks were set up on the Southern not only at all the London termini but at some fifteen suburban stations as well. The staff at each kiosk were kept up-to-date as to all train alterations on the line. They had the latest information by telephone from the various control offices and if the telephone broke down it was brought to them by a despatch rider. They had also the invaluable A.B.C. guide to help travellers as far as might be on their journeys over other lines. And they earned their living by the sweat of their brows. During the week ending 13 December 1941, a census was taken of the enquiries at the one and twenty kiosks in the London area and the total was, according to my arithmetic, 22,486. Charing Cross came first with over 4,500 and Waterloo a good second with over 3,700, but the suburban stations did nobly too with Wimbledon 1,139, Sutton 1,443 and Woolwich 1,505. Oddly enough the two lowest totals came from two London stations, Blackfriars and Holborn Viaduct. That the travellers at those two stations were so independent, or so incurious may seem odd, but the reason probably was that they were nearly all season-ticket holders and therefore well acquainted with the line. Those figures are sufficiently impressive but I must give just two more. In 1944 Charing Cross reached its peak with 8,000 questions answered in a week and during the same time the Central Telephone Enquiry Bureau at Waterloo answered 21,785." - Bernard Darwin

LOOKING AFTER THE PRESENT AND SAFEGUARDING THE PAST

Left - Looking after the present. Obviously a quiet day at Waterloo: judging from the 'Normal' notices on the board behind. This was one of several emergency canteens provided at Waterloo, and elsewhere, dispensing much needed foot - in quantity. No reference to ration books and coupons either, so it may have been early in WW2. The mention of cheesecake is interesting, somehow perceived as being a more recent innovation.

Above - Safeguarding the past. The former Bodmin & Wadebridge railway coach, previously on display at the terminus, being moved to safety 'for the duration. (With apologies for the marks on the negatives).

A PRELUDE TO AND THE RETURN FROM DUNKIRK

Above - On 13 December 1939, the German pocket battleship 'Graf Spee' was found by a British Naval Squadron off the Uruguay coast in what was to become the infamous Battle of the River Plate. Following heavy engagement, the enemy ship took refuge in neutral waters only to emerge again where she was scuttled by her Captain. Of the British vessels involved, both HMS Ajax and HMS Exeter were severely damaged, the latter such that she forced to break off the engagement to effect emergency repairs at Port Stanley. In addition to the damage to the ship, 63 of her company were killed and 23 wounded. The losses incurred on HMS Ajax were 5 killed and 7 wounded. HMS Exeter eventually returned to Plymouth in February 1940. Seen above is the scene at Waterloo on 27 February 1940 with the crews from both vessels the subject of much media attention prior to a planned morale boosting march through the City.

Opposite top - 'Peace in out time?' Almost a decade before the uttering of those infamous words, the first detachments of British Troops were elated on their arrival in England, after nearly eleven years occupation of the Rhine. The view shows a group from the Leicester Dorsetshire Regiments, venting their joy as they arrive at Waterloo Station in London 23 September 1929.

Opposite bottom - A decade later and it is still smiles all-round as the men from a Scottish Regiment prepare to travel to France. September 1939.

Above - The SR (formerly SECR) TSS Biarritz, one of numerous vessels commandeered by the Admiralty as troop transport and which saw service at both Dunkirk and later in connection with 'D-Day'. She is seen here off Folkestone.

Opposite top - The SS Antwerp at Southampton in June 1940. Notice the barrage balloons above the dock buildings. The negative packet for this illustration was marked 'Evacuation'.

Opposite bottom - A former LNER vessel, the SS Vienna, in use as a troopship. This was one of several ex-LNER ships which used Southern Railway ports during WW2. One quote from the period remarked, "SS Vienna was a name to strike fear in to the hearts of strong men when it was the one they were to travel on. It could turn a smooth sea into a typhoon struck ocean."

Above - Former LNER vessel the SS Amsterdam, commandeered and converted to a hospital ship as HMRS Amsterdam in 1939. She is seen here at Southampton but was subsequently lost off Dunkirk in August 1944 whilst evacuating wounded. 106 men perished.

Opposite page - French soldiers evacuated from Dunkirk seen at Dover and Margate, 4 June 1940. At this stage the station nameboard has not been removed to deter potential invaders.

Inset - emergency rations for those returning, the presence of the live rail will be noted. (Topic continued overleaf).

Operation 'Dynamo' and the necessary feeding of men, bedraggled, bemused and in many cases dispirited. The same could hardly be said of the railway staff, especially those at Headcorn, Paddock Wood and Tonbridge where food was provided - all sorts of delicacies being on offer from sandwiches, to jellied eels, sardines, cheese, oranges, hard boiled eggs, meat pies and sausages. The Tonbridge Station Master also organised collections: £1,000 was raised, whilst a tobacco manufacturer donated 60,000 cigarettes. One of the problems facing the im-

provised caterers was a shortage of drinking cups and recourse was made to tin cans. On the shout 'Sling em out', these receptacles were thrown out onto the platform as the train departed, ready to be collected, washed and made ready for the next arrival. Postcards too were distributed and collected, to be sent to families to assure those at home they were safe. At Penge there was similar bonhomie, with the local Salvation Army Band striking a resounding chorus as the trains passed through. Throughout all of this it was reported normal traffic, both passenger and freight, continued almost unaffected.

This page and opposite. Damaged stock at Bognor consequent upon the raid of 11 April 1941. Rather than having to rely solely upon photographic identification, the record tells us units, 1850, 2018, 2058, 2089, 2091, 2092, 3078, 3081, 3082, 3083 and 3145 were 'badly bombed'. Note the already restricted driver's window on No. 3145.

No similar record appears to exist for freight stock, as witness the damage to the vehicles seen on the opposite page which was recorded at Bognor on the same occasion. No doubt such a record would be of considerable size. The left hand side private-owner wagon at least would appear to be some way from home, bearing the ownership details: 'MOY' of Colchester.

UNITS AND STOCK DAMAGED BY ENEMY ACTION

John Atkinson

The following table is a list of incidents resulting from enemy action which are believed to have involved damage to electric stock during World War II. It was mainly compiled from records kept by Dick Coombes, but with supplementary support from documents within the National Archive (Kew).

Some of the units listed suffered only minor damage, such as broken windows and damaged panelling caused by shrapnel, but others were more seriously damaged by close proximity to or direct hits from, bombs, including V1 flying bombs and V2 rockets. Similarly damage may have been caused through a secondary source, such as derailment damage caused by encountering damaged tracks or debris on the lines.

There were several distinct phases of damage, although throughout the period 1940 to 1944 the South Coast and consequently Southern Railway territory, was subject to 'hit and run' raids. The first of these was in the Southampton area in June 1940.

The 'Battle of Britain', during 1940, mostly affected military targets, this however also included Naval installations, thus Southampton again, plus now Portsmouth, and Dover were all hit.

The concentrated 'blitz' on London lasted from early September 1940 until mid May 1941 and was when many of the London terminals and their approach tracks were damaged. The V1 flying bombs started to arrive from 13 June 1944, lasting until the end of October. They were followed by the V2 rockets from 8 September 1944 until March 1945. Additionally, there were many other minor instances of damage for which details are not fully known.

This list shows incidents in date order, the location affected, a brief description of the incident and the numbers of units known to have been affected, there may well have been others slightly damaged which have not been recorded. Unit numbers in italics are *possibly those involved*. Bomb types (where mentioned) as follows:-

A/A = Anti-aircraft shell
D/A = Delayed Action bomb
E/A = Enemy Action
F/B = Flying bomb (V1)
H/E = High Explosive bomb
I/B = Incendiary bomb
LRR = Long range rocket (V2)
M/C = Machine gun fire
O/B = Oil bomb
UXB = Unexploded bomb

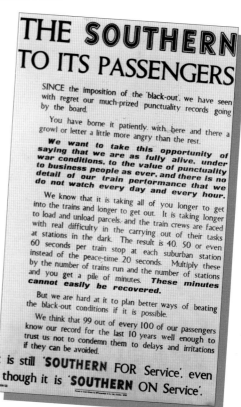

At 1.00 on Monday 14 October 1940 enemy planes dropped high explosive on the car sheds and sidings at Selhurst .

Six sidings and 'some electric stock was damaged'. Sidings 5 and 6 were not able to be restored until 3 April 1941, the rest until even later on 6 September 1941.

So quoted the official record, although the actual Southern Railway records refer to 6 vehicles being destroyed, 2 badly damaged and 10 slightly damaged. The units affected were Nos. 1170, 1044, 1139, 1170, 1184, 1259, 1426, 1785 and possibly No. 1697.

Below - The roof of 'Selhurst Cleaning Shed' on the same occasion.

DATE	TIME	LOCATION	DESCRIPTION	UNITS AFFECTED
12-8-40	?	Portsmouth Harbour	Seven coaches destroyed by I/B	2102, 2131, 3137
16-8-40	c17.30	Nr Hampton Wick	H/E blast, 2 bad & 11 slight	1517, 1145, 1516
			4 49 Wloo - Ted & 5 0 Shepp - Wloo	1476, 1131, 1237
31-8-40	?	Ford	Minor blast damage	2127
7-9-40	?	Falconwood	2 coaches damaged	1646
8-9-40	?	Victoria (E)	Empty train burned by I/B	1129, 1448
			3 burnt out, 2 damaged	
8-9-40	?	Wimbledon Park Sdgs	Berthed trains damaged by blast	1115, 1226, 1413, 1474, 1707
			11 slight	2024, 2107
8-9-40	?	Peckham Rye	Berthed stock damaged by I/B	1454, 1802
			2 burnt out, 3 damaged	
8-9-40	?	Clapham Yard	H/E blast, 2 slight	2043, 2119
9-9-40	17.50	Plumstead	Train hit by D/A, later exploded	1709, 1120, 1622
9-9-40	?	Dartford	H/E blast, 8 slight	1219, 1665, 1749, 1757
14-9-40	05.00	Westcombe Park	Unit damaged when station hit, 3 slight	1229
16-9-40	21.50	Tattenham Corner	3 car unit slightly damaged by I/B	?
16-9-40	22.20	Selhurst Depot	1 coach damaged by A/A shell	?
18-9-40	*?*	*?*	*1 destroyed, 1 slight*	*1038*
19-9-40	22.40	Charing Cross	H/E through roof, trailer set wrecked	*1063*
			in Platform 5	
20-9-40	00.55	Reigate	2-BIL in sidings damaged by blast debris	?
25-9-40	02.00	Waterloo	Waterloo & City Depot slight damage	?
			H/E in North Sidings, 3 compartments	
			of coach wrecked by flying wheelset	
			One coach in Plat 3 burnt by O/B	
25-9-40	?	Fratton Depot	Damaged by bombs	?
26-9-40	04.55	Herne Hill	6 car train badly damaged by H/E	?
27-9-40	05.40	Clapham Jct.	Empty stock derailed	?
27-9-40	03.48	Streatham Hill	Three coaches burnt by I/B	3073
27-9-40	09.48	Victoria	Bomb in Eastern Sidings	?
27-9-40	15.55	Herne Hill	H/E in sidings	?
30-9-40	08.10	Blackfriars	UXB through unit into river, 2 slight	1704
1-10-40	06.25	Maidstone Barracks	Berthed stock by H/E blast, 4 slight	1840, 2633
2-10-40	15.09	Peckham Rye Shops	Damaged by H/E	*2 x 6 car units*
7-10-40	19.45	Charing Cross	One compartment burnt by I/B	1715
8-10-40	08.48	Charing Cross	8 car train in Plat 5 bombed	?
			One MBT badly damaged	

Selhurst, 14 October 1940.

DATE	TIME	LOCATION	DESCRIPTION	UNITS AFFECTED
9-10-40	c20.00	Nr Bromley Jct.	Small fires in two MBTs, train	1634, 1638
			Bridging 'Dead section' after E/A	
9-10-40	22.25	Victoria	Station bombed. 1 bad, 1 slight	3052, 3134, 2611 + 2639
				1470 + 1081 + 1619
10-10-40	06.50	Surbiton	Train derailed by H/E blast	?
10-10-40	22.10	West Croydon	Train damaged when station hit by H/E	?
11-10-40	20.45	Bookham	Compartment burnt by I/B	?
14-10-40	01.25	Selhurst Depot	Insp. Shed hit by H/E	1009, 1044, 1139, 1170, 1184
			6 destroyed, 2 bad, 10 slight	1259, 1426, 1785, *1697*
14-10-40	20.23	London Bridge	Steam train derailed in bomb crater Central platforms also hit	-
14-10-40	23.31	Waterloo	One coach slight damage by I/B	1284
15-10-40	22.14	Durnsford Road	Power station hit by H/E	-
16-10-40	20.55	Waterloo	Two coaches damaged in Plat 3	?
16-10-40	23.24	Stewarts Lane	Shed hit by H/E, 4 coaches burnt out	?
16-10-40	*?*	*?*	*1 destroyed, 1 slight*	*1039*
17-10-40	19.35	New Cross Gate	Station hit by H/E, 3 slight	1430
17-10-40	22.20	Wimbledon Park Sdgs	Shed roof hit, stock slightly damaged	?
18-10-40	20.15	Selsdon	Electric train hit at Up Home	1283
			1 destroyed, 1 bad & 1 slight	
19-10-40	20.40	Nr Durnsford Road	Train hit by H/E, 2 coaches overturned	1530, *tlr*, 1439
			1 destroyed, 1 bad, 6 slight	

Two final views of the damage within Selhurst, showing left, the end of 1009 and below 1259. Whilst we have been privileged to have access to a considerable number of views relative to this time period, in proportionate terms only a few of the incidents within the table appear to have been photographed.

DATE	TIME	LOCATION	DESCRIPTION	UNITS AFFECTED
25-10-40	19.45	Orpington	Train hit by H/E passing Carr Shed	1745 + *tlr* + *3*
			Carr Sheds hit, 8 units + trailer set damaged. 3 destroyed	1473, 1501
26-10-40	15.30	Petts Wood	Train damaged by H/E blasts, 8 slight	1201, 1181, 1691
30-10-40	03.00	Selhurst Depot	Berthed stock burnt by I/B	1259, 1414, 1618
			1 destroyed, 8 slight	
2-11-40	10.20	Ravensbourne	2 coaches slight damage by blast	?
3-11-40	14.10	Alton	Cab slight damage by M/C	2062
4-11-40	19.25	Chelsfield	Footbridge dislodged onto train	*1760 + 1085*
			2 coaches badly damaged	
6-11-40	20.05	Gillingham Depot	Berthed train damaged, 8 slight	1419, 1134, 1521
11-11-40	16.15	Gatwick Airport	2 coaches roof damage by M/C	2949
11-11-40	21.20	Stone Crossing	Train ran into blast debris, minor damage	?
29-11-40	?	Tattenham Corner	Compartment burnt by I/B	?
"11-40"	?	?	*3 destroyed, 2 slight*	*1434*
"c11-40"	?	?	*1 destroyed, 1 slight*	*1159*
4-12-40	?	?	*2 destroyed*	*1055*
8-12-40	20.15	Hampton Court	7 coaches burnt out, 6 others damaged by	3058, 3059, 3070
			I/B 2 compts damaged in suburban units	? ?
8-12-40	20.15	London Bridge	I/Bs on roof of departing train	?
			2 coaches roofs burnt through	
8-12-40	?	W & City	Tunnels flooded, 12 week closure	?
9-12-40	02.00	Blackheath	Berthed train damaged by H/E blast	?
15-12-40	21.15	Reigate	Minor damage by A/A shell	2681
27-12-40	19.50	Knights Hill Tnl	Train hit debris within tunnel, MBT wrecked. Not removed until 20-1-41	?
29-12-40	18.30	London Bridge	Bad fire in Ctl side, berthed trains burnt	?
			Departing train hit by I/Bs	?
29-12-40	19.55	Holborn - Blackfriars	Bad fires, berthed stock at Blackfriars hit	?
			by I/Bs	
7-1-41	13.01	Clapham Junction	2 Compts burnt by I/B	1206
10-1-41	19.10	Fratton Depot	Various coaches damaged in yard	?
10-1-41	21.35	Portsmouth Harbour	13 coaches burnt out,	3060, 3117, 3119
			3 others damaged by I/B	3132
11-1-41	21.15	Blackfriars	Two MBT badly damaged by H/E	?
11-1-41	20.30	Waterloo	One coach damaged by I/B	1666
2-3-41	06.30	W&C	Line reopened peak hours only	-
15-3-41	23.00	Peckham Rye	H/E in sidings, stock damaged by blast	?
19-3-41	21.40	New Cross Gate	Badly bombed, 2x8 suburban	?
			1x4Lav, 1x4Cor 2x2Bil damaged	

DATE	TIME	LOCATION	DESCRIPTION	UNITS AFFECTED
8-4-41	22.30	Fratton	One MBT burnt out	3116
11-4-41	23.10	Bognor Regis	Badly bombed	1850, 2018 2058, 2089, 2091, 2092, 3078, 3081, 3082, 3083, 3085
16-4-41	22.40	Belvedere	Rear coach of train derailed	?
17-4-41	02.10	Eardley Sidings	Several withdrawn W&C coaches burnt by I/B	?
17-4-41	02.45	Charing Cross	Station hit by I/B, 4 trains on fire 4 destroyed, 2 bad (+ others)	1612, 1722 ? ?
17-4-41	03.25	Victoria	12 coaches damaged	?
17-4-41	Overnight	Beckenham Junction	Berthed stock damaged by H/E blast	?
17-4-41	22.37	Fratton Depot	Shed damaged	?
19-4-41	23.53	Elmers End	Berthed stock damaged by H/E blast	?
20-4-41	03.55	Streatham Hill	Some electric stock destroyed	?
25-4-41	07.25	Lancing Works	Hit by H/E, 1 destroyed, 2 bad	1305
26-4-41	22.00	Ports & Southsea	20 coaches damaged by blast	?
27-4-41	23.00	Fratton Depot	3 coaches burnt out by I/B	3144
3-5-41	22.30	Fratton Depot	1 coach burnt out by I/B	2145
4-5-41	20.58	Ports S'sea DCS	D/A explosion, 1 destroyed, 1 bad	1828
11-5-41	01.00	London Bridge Ctl	8car & 4☐BIL H/E blast	?
11-5-41	03.15	Elmers End	H/E hit, 1 destroyed, 2 bad	1799
11-5-41	03.55	Cannon Street	2x8 cars slight damage by I/B	?
11-5-41	Overnight	Plumstead	2x8cars H/E blast	?
"7-41"	?	?	*4 bad & 6 slight*	*1825, 3112, 3149*
4-5-42	13.50	Eastbourne	Station hit by H/E, 8 bad & 2 slight	1835, 1840, 3029
7-5-42	15.10	Eastbourne	Station hit by H/E, 2 slight	1816
9-5-42	06.19	Galley Hill - Bexhill	Train hit by M/C, 4 slight	2066, 2069
18-5-42	20.06	Brighton	Works hit by H/E, debris on station 4 bad & 4 slight	2019, 2039, 2046 2150, 2632
9-8-42	14.00	Littlehampton	H/E blast, 2 slight	2126
11-8-42	23.15	Eastbourne	Station hit by H/E. 1 coach derailed 2 bad & 6 slight	2093, 2114, 2646 2686
14-8-42	15.05	Bognor Regis	H/E blast, 2 slight	3104, 3133
19-8-42	?	Fratton	H/E blast, 1 slight	3109
30-9-42	12.15	Lancing Works	Works bombed 2 bad & 16 slight	1256, 1485, 1507, 1776, 1833, 1847, 3004
12-10-42	12.26	Brighton	H/E blast, 2 slight	2091
4-11-42	12.40	Seaford	H/E blast, 4 slight	1823, 1844

A landmine dropped on the night of 12 December 1940 'resting' but now rendered safe, at the base of the signal box at London Bridge - the signalman continued working.

DATE	TIME	LOCATION	DESCRIPTION	UNITS AFFECTED
"1942"	*?*	*?*	*1 bad & 3 slight*	*3080*
"1942"	*?*	*?*	*?*	*1428, 1432, 1475*
20-1-43	?	London Bridge	?, 1 slight	1668
20-1-43	12.45	Three Bridges	Berthed unit by M/C, 1 slight	2924
22-1-43	?	?	*H/E blast?*, 1 slight	1699
3-3-43	c20.30	Putney - Barnes	Train hit by falling debris, 2 slight	1468
4-3-43	04.56	Gravesend Central	*H/E blast?*, 2 slight	1481, 1619
7-3-43	12.55	Eastbourne	Station hit by H/E, 4 slight	1843, 2005
			(12 12 Ore to Btn [1843] blast,	
			2005 berthed, roof damage)	
9-3-43	16.55	West Worthing	3.25 Vic - Lit train hit by M/C, 4 slight	3030
19-4-43	01.15	New Cross Gate	H/E blast, 1 slight	1762
18-5-43	?	Dartford	*H/E blast?*, 1 slight	1739
23-5-43	13.02	Bexhill	H/E blast, 1 slight	2937

DATE	TIME	LOCATION	DESCRIPTION	UNITS AFFECTED
25-5-43	12.21	Brighton	Depot and Pullman shops hit and span of London Road viaduct demolished by H/E, 3 coaches wrecked, 3 badly damaged and 75 others with lesser damage.	1814, 1821, 1822, 1827, 1831, 2011, 2014, 2030, 2036, 2046, 2063, 2088, 2145, 2927, 2928, 2931, 2934, 2935, 2952, 3011, 3015, 3019, 3022, 3028, 3030, 3032, 3033, 3041, *'Bertha'*, *'Brenda'*, *'Ethel'*, *'Gladys'*, *'Joyce'*, *May'*, *'Olive'*, *'Rita'*, *'Rose'*, *'Ruth'*, *'Violet'*.
4-6-43	11.28	Eastbourne	H/E blast, 2 slight	1833
18-8-43	22.45	Southease - Newhaven	H/E blast, 1 slight	3017

This page and opposite - Brighton in consequence of the raid of 25 May 1943. This was the second raid on the railway here in just a week, an earlier bombing raid of 18 May (see pages 90/91), had damaged the works and associated machinery, but not it seems, any rolling stock.

On 25 May though it was different, five bombs fell, some causing the major amount of damage referred to in the table opposite (which included the Preston Park Works of the Pullman Company), whilst by an unlucky fluke one of the devices fell in the vicinity of a supporting brick pier at the Brighton end of the viaduct between the station and London Road. The actual bomb had completely passed through a residential property before exploding against the brick pier, the rails left dangling some 67 feet above the ground. Regretfully, because of the number of houses in the vicinity, the raid took a heavy toll in casualties, 24 were killed and 130 injured.

Within a matter of days the debris had been cleared, scaffolding erected and a temporary steel support provided to allow both lines to re-open. The timescale involved before the temporary structure was ready is subject to different reports, but it was between one and five weeks. Again, despite the amount of stock damage, no other views of the railway have been uncovered.

This page - 29 June 1943 and final tests are under way on the new, temporary structure. Two 'H1' class '*Atlantics*', Nos. 2037 '*Selsey Bill*' and 2041 '*Peveril Point*' are involved, having a combined weight in the order of 212 tons.

Opposite - 1 July 1943 and reported as 'Trains running', although it cannot confirmed if this was in fact the first service train to cross the new structure. At this stage the scaffolding was still in place although it was finally removed in September 1943. The engine is a 4-4-2T, on a Tonbridge to Brighton, via Eridge service.

UNITS AND STOCK DAMAGED BY ENEMY ACTION

DATE	TIME	LOCATION	DESCRIPTION	UNITS AFFECTED
16-9-43	?	Gillingham	*H/E blast?*, 1 slight	2614
7-10-43	?	Gillingham	*H/E blast?*, 1 slight	1688
22-10-43	03.46	Kemp Town	H/E blast, 2 slight	3034
"c1943"	?	?	?	*1774*
29-1-44	?	Gillingham	4 coaches damaged by I/B, 4 slight	2601, 2623, 2649, 2676
4-2-44	05.45	Slades Green	2 coaches wrecked, 34 damaged by H/E blast	1006, 1139, 1168, 1230, 1251, 1286, 1433, 1484, 1502, 1621 1683, 1729, 1741, 1788, 3030
14-2-44	?	London Bridge	*H/E blast?*, 1 slight	1787
19-2-44	01.05	Wimbledon Park Sdgs	H/E blast, 1 slight	3142
20-2-44	?	Spa Road	H/E blast, 9 slight	1001, 1490, 1519, 1617
21-2-44	?	East Putney	Roof burnt by I/B, 1 slight	2134
23-2-44	22.40	Hampton Wick	Train damaged by I/B, 2 slight	1602
23-2-44	22.50	Redhill - Earlswood	Unex. A/A shell, 1 slight	2948
24-2-44	22.00	Herne Hill	H/E blast, 2 slight	993
24-2-44	22.05	Loco Jct, Vauxhall	Train damaged by blast from H/E (9 59pm Wloo - H Ct) 1 destroyed, 4 bad & 3 slight	1712, 1061, 1784

DATE	TIME	LOCATION	DESCRIPTION	UNITS AFFECTED
24-2-44	22.10	Wimbledon Park Sdgs	A/A shell, 1 slight	2075
26-2-44	?	Aldershot	??, 1 slight	2074
2-3-44	03.05	Streatham Hill	Compt. burnt by I/B	2005
2-3-44	03.20	Strood	Shoebeam bkn by H/E blast	1503
14-3-44	01.00	Eastbourne	H/E blast, 1 slight	1827
14-3-44	23.10	Waterloo	Shrapnel, 1 slight	4139
22-3-44	?	Wimbledon Park Sdgs	??, 1 slight	2051
25-3-44	00.05	Beckenham Jct.	A/A shell, 2 slight	1618
16-6-44	05.35	Addiscombe	F/B blast, 1 slight	1860
16-6-44	07.37	Welling	F/B blast, 1 slight	1586
16-6-44	09.05	Lower Sydenham	Shrapnel, 1 slight	1604
17-6-44	?	Brighton	F/B blast, 1 slight	2949
17-6-44	03.20	Tattenham Corner	F/B blast, 4 slight	1515, 1580, 1656
17-6-44	03.26	West Croydon	F/B blast, 3 bad & 5 slight	1509, 1740, 1880
18-6-44	04.10	Charing Cross	F/B blast, 1 bad & 6 slight	1104, 1293, 1796
18-6-44	?	Victoria	F/B blast, 1 slight	2673
19-6-44	08.38	Raynes Park	8 L/S/L bkn by F/B blast, 5 slight	2034, 2114, 2677
21-6-44	14.10	Clock House	17 windows bkn by F/B blast, 7 slight	1524, 1051, 1594
22-6-44	07.03	Forest Hill	F/B blast, 7 slight	1626, 1012, 1782
22-6-44	c18.35	Kemsing - Otford Jct.	A/A shell wrecked 4compts.	2654
22-6-44	?	Wimbledon	F/B blast, 1 slight	4149
23-6-44	01.58	West Croydon	Berthed stock by F/B blast 1 dest, 1 bad, 28 slight	1026, 1031, 1065, 1180, 1434, 1527, 1529, 1621, 1628, 1640, 1679, 1704, 1799, 1854
23-6-44	06.58	Windmill Bdge Jct.	F/B blast, 4 bad & 4 slight	2933, 2944
23-6-44	09.34	Waterloo	19 coaches slightly damaged by F/B blast	W&C 82, 1412, 1424, 1587, 4250, 4251
23-6-44	*?*	*????*	*?*	*1590*
25-6-44	01.56	Victoria	F/B blast, 3 slight	1475
27-6-44	?	Waterloo	F/B blast, 1 slight	?
28-6-44	22.50	Walworth	F/B blast, 1 dest & 2 slight	1728
29-6-44	10.32	Wimbledon Park Sdgs	F/B hit, 3 dest & 5 slight	3063, 3101
30-6-44	01.15	Bickley	F/B hit, 5 dest & 19 slight	1598, 1692 + ?
30-6-44	10.25	Streatham Hill	F/B blast, 2 slight	?
1-7-44	02.59	Victoria	F/B blast, 10 slight	2633, 265, 2674, 2952
1-7-44	12.20	Greenwich	F/B blast, 5 bad & 3 slight (11 48am Dart - Charing Cross)	?
1-7-44	13.00	Shortlands	F/B blast, 5 slight (12 31pm HV - SV)	1222, 1873, 1251

Wooden bodied rolling stock following the attack near Bramley, near Guildford, 16 December 1942. (- see next page)

DATE	TIME	LOCATION	DESCRIPTION	UNITS AFFECTED
1-7-44	14.46	Streatham Hill	F/B blast, 11 bad (2.37pm S. Hill - VIC)	5-Pul / 6-Pan *3034*
1-7-44	15.00	Bickley Jn	F/B blast, 8 slight	1744, 1051, 1626
1-7-44	23.33	Waterloo	F/B blast, 2 slight	4133
			(11.31pm Wloo - Straw Hill)	
2-7-44	02.15	New Cross Gate	38 coaches damaged by F/B blast	2634, 2643, 2610, 2602, 1685,
				1487, 2936, 2925, 1647, 1128,
				1522, 1299, 1054, 1747,

Seven people were killed when a two-coach passenger train travelling from Guildford to Horsham was attacked by a German plane at Bramley on the afternoon of 16 December 1942. The two-coach train was busier than usual with the regular commuters joined by other passengers who had been Christmas shopping in Guildford.

The enemy plane, believed to have been a Dornier, dropped a stick of bombs as the train was pulling away from Bramley station and passing close to the Home signal. According to a report in the *Surrey Times* of 19 December, the train did not receive a direct hit, as the bombs struck the railway embankment. However the impact and consequent concussion was severe enough to rip open the side of one carriage while badly damaging the other. The presence of a corridor on one side may have meant the number of casualties was fortunately less than it might have been. Neither was there a derailment.

Those killed or fatally injured included the Driver, George Budd, and the Guard George Jeal. The Fireman, Fairey by name, was the only person out of 20 on the train who was not injured. He had seen the plane approaching and crouched down next to the coal bunker. Even so the force of one of the explosions: (there were at least four HE bombs), threw him backwards covering him with dirt. Another passenger, travelling in one of the compartments where there were fatalities, was lifted from the seat and blown through the carriage window from the force of the explosion.

As was invariably the case, assistance was at first limited. Fortunately Fireman Fairey was a member of the award winning Horsham First Aid team and he single-handed attended the dying and injured until help, in the form of six Canadian soldiers, a Doctor and ARP services arrived.

The injured were taken by ambulance to Guildford Hospital whilst troops were later drafted in to assist in clearing the debris: made more difficult as it was at first thought there might be two further UXBs in the vicinity. Of the bombs that caused the devastation, one had passed clean through the two front windows of a pair of cottages, wrecking the furniture before ricocheting off the ground and on to the railway. Fireman Fairey also reported for duty as usual the next day. (The identity of the locomotive was not reported).

(With due acknowledgement to 'Guildford The War Years' - Breedon Books.)

Damaged stock at Bramley. The debris on the solebar is that thrown up from the impact. Notice the evidence of bullet holes as well.

DATE	TIME	LOCATION	DESCRIPTION	UNITS AFFECTED
4-7-44	08.55	St Helier - Morden Sth	F/B blast, 4 slight	1688, 1056
			(8.41am Wall - HV)	
4-7-44	08.50	Waterloo	F/B blast, 4 slight	1719, 1178, 1656
			(8.17am Chess - Wloo)	
4-7-44	10.03	Wimbledon Park Sdgs	F/B blast, 2 bad & 74 slight	1278, 1496+ ?
5-7-44	18.10	Victoria	F/B blast, 1 slight	?
7-7-44	14.35	New Cross Gate	F/B blast, 22 bad & 19 slight	3043, 8x2cars, 4x3cars, 2x4cars

DATE	TIME	LOCATION	DESCRIPTION	UNITS AFFECTED
10-7-44	19.35	Bromley South	F/B blast, 7 slight (6 51pm HV - SV [7])	1461, 1182, 1751
11-7-44	18.10	Crystal Palace LL	Units slight damage by F/B blast	1861, 1875
14-7-44	08.50	Selhurst	F/B blast, 3 bad & 11 slight (8 9am Ep Dns - Vic [?] & 8 31am Vic - C.Nth [?])	1733, 1186, 1715 1629, 1079, 1413
15-7-44	13.50	London Bridge	F/B blast, 2 slight (1 40pm CX - Hayes [2])	1230
16-7-44	19.24	Clapham Junction	F/B blast, 6 slight (6 28pm Tatt - Vic [6])	1446, 1677
21-7-44	13.22	Earlsfield	F/B blast, 1 slight (1 7pm Wloo - Dkg [1])	1079
21-7-44	04.45	New Cross Gate	F/B blast, 24 damaged	?
23-7-44	04.10	Cannon Street	F/B blast, 10 slight	1664, 1071, 1675, 1502, 1605, 1133
"7-44"	?	? (probably NXG)	?	2950, 2954
2-8-44	14.15	New Cross Gate	F/B blast, 1 slight	?
2-8-44	13.00	Plumstead	F/B blast, 2 slight	1296
4-8-44	19.04	Motspur Park	F/B blast, 3 slight (6 47pm Wloo - Eff Jct.)	?
6-8-44	03.50	London Bridge	F/B blast, 4 slight (7 4am LBge - Ore [1] & 7 18am LBge - Ep Dns [3])	2942 1751
6-8-44	17.04	West Dulwich	Train damaged when station hit	?
6-8-44	17.10	Sydenham Hill	F/B blast, 7 slight (3 49pm Maid E - Vic [1] & 4 54pm Vic - Orp [6])	? ? ?
8-8-44	?	Crystal Palace	F/B blast, 2 stored buffet cars	? ?
16-8-44	18.31	NXG - Brockley	F/B blast, 8 slight (6 24pm LB - Couls N.)	?
21-8-44	20.45	Strawberry Hill	F/B blast, 11 slight	1149, 1169, 1672, 1698, 4151, 4219
23-8-44	c21.00	Herne Hill	F/B blast, 5 slight (8 43pm HV - Wall & 2 in sidings)	1303, 1688
"8-44"	?	?	?	3153
24-9-44	21.55	Chertsey	F/B blast, 8 slight	4132, 4197
26-10-44	08.40	Nr Sth Bermondsey	F/B blast, 3 dest, 2 bad & 5 slight (7 47am LBge - LBge [3] & 08.31 LBge - LBge [3 dest, 2 bad, 2 slight])	1793 1267, 1023, 1268

DATE	TIME	LOCATION	DESCRIPTION	UNITS AFFECTED
1-11-44	18.30	Nr Brockley	LRR blast, 1 bad & 9 slight (4 58pm Btn - LBge [5] & 5 45pm LBge - LBge [1 bad 4 slight])	1466, 1193, 1668 2054, 2078, 2949
11-11-44	01.53	Beckenham Junction	LRR blast, 5 slight	1849, 1715
14-11-44	06.20	Nr Petts Wood	LRR blast, 7 slight	1423, 1849, 1450
14-11-44	08.35	Eltham Well Hall	LRR blast, 8 slight	1478, 999, 1413
25-11-44	12.20	New Cross Gate	LRR blast, 2 coaches wrecked	*1138*
"1944"	?	?	?	*2107, 2938, 3128*
6-1-45	22.46	Peckham Rye Shed	LRR hit, 2 coaches destroyed, 7 bad damage, 11 lesser damage	1065, 1109, *1807*, 1427, 1428, *1483*, 2119
24-1-45	16.18	Greenwich	Train derailed by debris (4 14pm CSt - Gill.)	2656
7-3-45	08.35	Westcombe Park	LRR blast (minor dam)	?
8-3-45	12.05	Blackheath	LRR blast	1525, 995, 1776
14-3-45	?	Waterloo	LRR blast	4139
"1945"	?	?	?	*3054, 3130*
Unknown	?	?	?	*1417, 1437, 2947, 3074, 3148*
				3150

The Ivy Arch pedestrian tunnel under the railway at Worthing, as seen from Station Road, circa 1944.
West Sussex Museum Service PP/WSL/WGP000028

42

LOCOMOTIVES AND MANUFACTURING

Arguably the best known of all work undertaken by the SR workshops during WW2 were the building of 18 'Merchant Navy' class locomotives at Eastleigh between 1941 and 1944. Classified at the time as 'mixed-traffic', their very construction was the subject of some unrest amongst the workforce in 1941, who felt the effort could have been better spent on more obvious war work. In the view above, 21C5 *'Canadian Pacific'* is seen in the works yard at Eastleigh, probably brand new, in December 1941.

Left, 21C9 *'Shaw Savill'* leaves Waterloo on 6 May 1943, for the West of England with 16 coaches of 516 tons and seating for 900 passengers.

21C10 in plain black and at this stage un-named, later *'Blue Star'*, reported as on a trial run, leaving Waterloo with 20 coaches, 2 December 1942. This particular trial was one relating to haulage capacity and fuel consumption, several such workings taking place in 1941/42 when services of 18 and 20 coaches were taken between Waterloo and Exeter, also 17 coaches from Waterloo to Bournemouth West. Although certainly within the capabilities of the locomotive, such long trains were difficult for the operators to deal with, often blocking access to adjacent platforms. Several other members of the 'Merchant Navy' class were involved in these tests, including 21C3, 21C3, and 21C4.

A SUMMARY

It was reported that during the War years, the Southern Railway recorded 14 bridges demolished, 42 seriously damaged and 143 less seriously damaged. To repair them 46,500 cubic yards of filling material, 1,904 tons of steel girders, 650 tons of steel trestling and an incredible 109,600 feet of shoring timber was used.

Meanwhile at Ashford, the Bulleid / Raworth electric locomotive CC1 had been completed and just two days later was recorded undergoing trials on the Brighton line: later load trials of passenger stock and 80 wagon freight trains would be taken. The shielded windows were a wartime necessity

During the worst of the Blitz, from September 1940 to May 1941, 123 bomb incidents occurred on just one section of SR, that between Charing Cross and Cannon Street to New Cross and New Cross Gate, whilst 62 incidents were reported between Holborn Viaduct and Herne Hill.

From 'Purley Days' - edited by David Monk-Steel

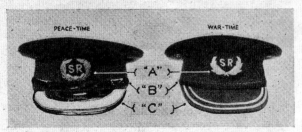

THE "AUSTERITY" CAP: The adoption by the Company of a new pattern cap for Stationmasters and Inspectors will effect a saving of 200 yards of heavy gold braid and 12½ pounds of gold wire, straps and buttons. "A" shows gold braid on badge replaced by cotton, "B" disappearance of leather straps and buttons, "C" heavy gold braid on peak reduced to two single lines and leather peak replaced by cloth.

Above - Forty 0-6-0 locomotives of the Q1 type were built to a Bulleid design at Brighton and Ashford between March and December 1942. Functional, if unconventional in appearance, they served a useful need.

Left - Also very much 'Austerity' in design, it has to be admitted that the 'no frills' style was present on the Southern not just in locomotive building either: as witness the 'Austerity' cap.

Top - The marks on the negative are unfortunate but do not detract from what is possibly the first time an illustration of the design has been seen with the 'Southern' identification high on the tender side - on subsequent engines it was placed more centrally. Interestingly also, both this and the plate carrying the number would appear to be of thin metal attached to the sides. Brighton, March 1942. Later, transfers / paint was used.

Bottom - An official view of No.C1 included for comparative purposes with conventional lettering and position

Above and left - The results of enemy action during an attack at Ashford Works, 28 November 1942. 'Q1' No. C34, one of three of the type completed at the Kent works during that month, has received a small amount of bullet damage to the boiler side and tender. Ashford Works was just seven minutes flying time from enemy air fields in northern France. On this occasions it is believed casualties had been light, although not so a few weeks earlier, when, on 26 October several of the shops were damaged and 11 workers killed. (The same raid of 28 November has seen a 'lucky' bullet strike the cab beading of 'N' class No. 1403 severing the pep-pipe. Some other shrapnel damage also occurred).

Jeremy Cobb collection

Bottom left - All the Southern workshops had their own ARP arrangements and requisite wardens, those seen being from Eastleigh.

Howard Butler collection

Right - Inside Eastleigh Works and the result of an unfortunate accident, not this time due to enemy action. It would seem that in the course of lifting the side-tank onto the framing of 'D1' No 2262, it slipped, injuring Erector W A G Follett and Plater J G Watkinson, 21 July 1941.

John Wenyon collection

Opposite top - Stanier design 8F, No. 8600, one of 23 of the class built at Eastleigh, seen here at the place of its birth. Each carried a suitably inscribed builders plate. Construction had started in early 1942 and by 1943 Brighton had completed loco No. 8645, the fiftieth to be built at the Sussex works. A further 14 were made at Ashford, making a total of 130 by the SR.

Opposite bottom - WD 2-8-0 No. 7422 at Nine Elms, 31 January 1944. At this time several of the type were working on the Southern Railway.

This page top - A visitor at Eastleigh, US Transportation Co. 2-8-0 No. 1843 recorded in Hampshire on 16 April 1943.

Above - As war progressed, so the cab side windows of many classes were blanked out in an attempt to reduce glare. Rails were also hung between the cab and tender on which black-out curtains could be attached. . 'Schools' No. 930 *'Radley'* is seen as such on 21 March 1941. For the time being the engine still retains malachite livery. From April 1942, shortage of materials meant engines passing through works were repainted in plain black. The presence of polished buffers on No. 930 would indicate some form of special working. **Inset** - 'Lord Nelson' No. 856 *'Lord St. Vincent'* in wartime guise.

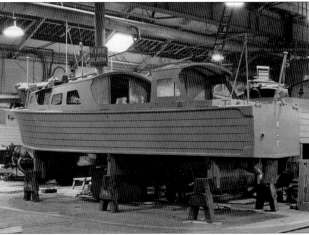

This page - War work of a different kind at Eastleigh, with construction of Naval '30ft fast motor-boats' (this page top and centre right and bottom left) and landing craft (top left and centre left). This construction was completed in the carriage shops. All were recorded in April 1942. Parts of the Carriage Works were also given over to Aircraft construction, many women being employed on this task.

Opposite - Completed naval equipment, that at top certainly wide of gauge at present, although they were turned at an angle before moving any distance. At bottom, With the Carriage Works in the background, '02' No. 230 has charge of five armoured hulls ready for fitting out. In addition to naval work, Eastleigh was responsible for part construction and then assembly of Matilda Tanks*. On occasions these would give demonstrations of their prowess in a nearby field, "...it rushed around with its bridge folded in half until it reaches the edge of a pit some 30 feet wide. Here it stops while the bridge rises, and slowly unfolds itself. It bridges the pit and at the same time detaches itself from the tank, which then crosses the pit, picks up the bridge again and goes on its way…".

John Wenyon and Tim Stubbs collections.

* Strictly speaking not a tank but an 'AVRE' (Armoured Vehicle Royal Engineers). It was based on a Matilda tank hull, but instead of the turret and gun, had the folding bridge as described.

The locomotive and carriage works at Eastleigh in 1944.

The views were taken in consequence of the visit of a Turkish delegation. 'Schools' No 914 *'Eastbourne'* is in the process of repair.

TROUBLE WITH ENGINES AND DEPOTS

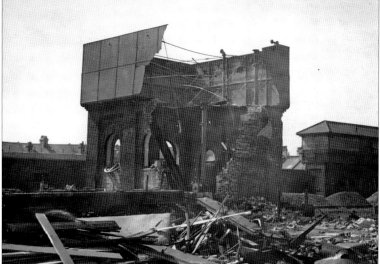

The seaside town of Eastbourne was an unfortunate regular target of enemy hit and run raids. Mostly these affected the town and municipal buildings, the intention of course to demoralise the populace. On 4 May 1942 it was the railway's turn, with considerable damage to the engine shed and water tower. Whilst the water tower was repaired, the shed roof never was, although the framework would survive until 1969. In addition to damage to the loco department, there was damage to rolling stock - as described on page 31.

A few months later, on 16 September 1942, a demonstration of a motor fire pump was being given by an Inspector to the railway staff, when a raider flashed over. The Inspector and several of the staff were killed and the pump wrecked.

Jeremy Cobb collection

Above - It is convenient then, even if slightly out of subject order, to deal with Eastbourne in one go, that above showing the effect on the station of the raid of 4 May 1942 which took place around 1.50 pm. High explosive was involved with vehicles badly damaged and two slightly damaged. The electric stock involved were unit Nos. 1835, 1840, 3029

Opposite page - Next we see the scene on Platforms 3 and 4 on 10 August 1942. (The damaged stock register on page 31 refers to 11 August at 11.15 pm.) Whatever, again high explosive was involved and one coach derailed. Units 2093, 2114 and 2646 were damaged.

Pages 56/57 overleaf - Reported as noon 16 September 1942 (although possibly the main view at least referred to 10 August 1942), the aftermath of when several staff were killed, as described on the previous page. This time there is damage to the station, stock and yard although no mention of EMU stock damage.

This page - An unidentified ex SECR 'E' class 4-4-0 in consequence of the raid on Ashford Works and Loco depot of 24 March 1943. Following on just months after the area had been previously hit, see page 48, this raid resulted in a quarter of the erecting shop being placed out of action. Eight were killed and 41 injured. Considerable damage was also wrought in the town itself. (On 11 December 1942, at least one engine 'L' No. 1772 received shrapnel damage in another incident at the same location).

Opposite - Scenes from the same raid. The 'Mogul': possibly an 'N1' is not identified, although below is 'C' class No. 1588. All were repaired and returned to traffic.   Jeremy Cobb collection

Left - What would be classified as a minor incident. 'King Arthur' No.793 *'Sir Ontzlake'* with machine gun and cannon shell holes through the boiler and cab at Sandwich, 10 May 1941.

Jeremy Cobb and RCHS collections

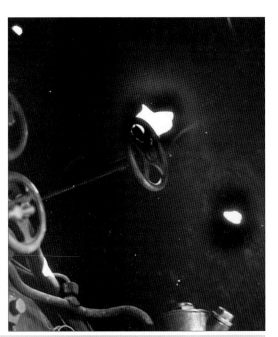

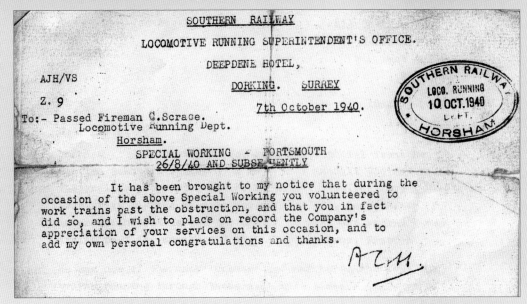

SOUTHERN RAILWAY

LOCOMOTIVE RUNNING SUPERINTENDENT'S OFFICE.

DEEPDENE HOTEL,

AJH/VS

DORKING. SURREY

Z.9

7th October 1940.

To:- Passed Fireman C.Scrace.
Locomotive Running Dept.
Horsham.
SPECIAL WORKING - PORTSMOUTH
26/8/40 AND SUBSEQUENTLY

It has been brought to my notice that during the occasion of the above Special Working you volunteered to work trains past the obstruction, and that you in fact did so, and I wish to place on record the Company's appreciation of your services on this occasion, and to add my own personal congratulations and thanks.

Above - New Cross sometime in 1944. In steam in the background is one of the 'D' class tank converted to act as a mobile fire-pump. At 12.26 pm on 25 November 1944, a rocket fell near here, damaging windows and roofs at the adjacent station , signal box, depot and workshop. Some debris also fell on the up local line but this was cleared in little more than 10 minutes. Two male members of staff were killed and two female carriage cleaners were never seen again. If it believed they may have been in the nearby Woolworth's store which took the direct hit. 168 were killed and 121 injured in what was the worst tragedy involving a V2 rocket.

Opposite bottom - On pages 37/40 of the first book 'Wartime Southern', reference was made to the unexploded bomb near Fratton and how some crews volunteered to pass it - notwithstanding it was till live. Passed Fireman C Scrace was one of those men, and who subsequently received a letter of thanks.

His son, the railway photographer, John Scrace, adds slightly more to the human element involved, "I remember him telling me how some footplate crews hung out on the 'safe' side of the engine when passing the bomb, whilst one Guard, apparently too frightened to remain in his van at the rear of the goods train, opted to join his colleagues on the engine, 'unofficially' of course - only for the fireman to strike the side of the tender an almightily bang with his shovel at the precise spot where the bomb was located".

A conflict of information now. We can be certain the engine is 'Schools' No. 917 *'Ardingly'*, what we cannot be certain of is exactly where and when the damage was caused. On the reverse of the prints and on the negative packet was the reference, 'Deal Station, E.A. (Enemy Action) 11 August 1942'. According to D L Bradley, this engine was attacked by cannon shells near Ramsgate shed on 21 August 1942. The damage was not too serious with only the smokebox penetrated. The fireman however was injured as he hurriedly left the footplate falling heavily on to the track. Reports elsewhere have the engine receiving works attention from 12 September 1942 to 27 January 1943.   Jeremy Cobb and RCHS collections

One of the best known incidents involving a Southern engine in WW2 occurred on Romney Marsh, near the station of Lydd Town, 28 November 1942*. 'D3' 0-4-4T No 2365 was in charge of the afternoon New Romney - Ashford passenger working about a mile north of Lydd, when it was attacked by cannon fire from a low flying enemy aircraft. At least one shell hit and ruptured the boiler. The resultant mass of escaping steam - and bits of locomotive being flung in all several directions, may well have disorientated the pilot as he crashed , and was killed, about 100 yards from the line. It has often been recounted that it was the resultant mass of escaping steam and debris travelled upwards that was the cause of the pilot loosing control: being barely 20 feet above the train. Other reports though refer to the pilot misjudging his height and catching his left wingtip on the cab roof. Whatever, both the engine crew, albeit understandably badly shaken, survived. The locomotive taken to a siding at Lydd Town where the majority of the accompanying photographs were taken. Despite the apparent extreme damage, it was towed to Ashford and after a spare boiler had been fitted, returned to traffic, surviving until September 1952.

* The dates of 26 and 27 November have also been mentioned.

Above - No. 2365 awaiting recovery to Ashford whilst various parts litter the surrounding fields. At top right is the dome cover, centre right: the dome itself, and bottom right, a side tank.　　Jeremy Cobb and RCHS collections

This page right and opposite - On 18 November 1942, when little more than a year old, 'Merchant Navy' No. 21C4 *'Cunard White Star'* was heading a goods train near Whimple when it was attached by a low flying enemy bomber. Whilst some shells did hit the locomotive, it was two covered vans immediately next to the tender that took the full blast and immediately burst into flames. The train was stopped, parted, and the engine crew together with the guard attempted to fight the blaze as best as possible until assistance arrived. No. 21C4 was photographed a few days later at Exmouth Junction with much of its casing removed, no doubt to check for damage, before being taken away for repairs. The impact marks made by the enemy action on the various locomotive parts, as well as the blank of the side window will be noted. What has not been stated, as yet, was the content of the vehicles that caught fire; bacon and ham. The fact both foods were by now severely rationed would have done little to cool the tempers of the men involved subjected to such aroma and yet unable to partake. After repair, the loco subsequently returned to its then home shed of Exmouth Junction.

Jeremy Cobb collection

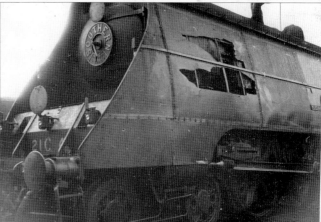

The depot at Tunbridge Wells was visited by the enemy on 20 November 1940. Aside from working locomotives, the shed had at times played host to a number of stored 4-4-2Ts, although whether any of those seen were at the time in this category cannot be confirmed. Clearly blast damage has occurred, sufficient to physically lift and then move sideways a 60 ton locomotive. The bomb then passed through into the supporting arches beneath. Unseen from the views, but totally understandable, was that the shed roof was severely damaged, although unlike at Eastbourne, repairs were made with corrugated sheet: a covering that remained until closure.

One other engine, believed to be a C2 or C2X, is in steam on the right. The front of the tank engine on the extreme left having already been propped to prevent it falling further and possibly wreaking further havoc.

Already relegated to lesser duties, all but one of the 'I3' class survived WW2, those seen being repaired. The exception was No. 2024 condemned in 1944, not because of enemy attention, but because of its generally poor condition.

At the start of WW2, Nos. 2021 and 2024 were classed as in store at Tunbridge Wells, although around the time of the Battle of Britain, Nos. 2021, 2024, 2090 and 2091 were dis-

persed to store in a supposedly hidden siding at Hildenbrough, the idea being that should a main depot be attacked, not all might be lost. Incidentally, No. 2077 spent some time stored and surrounded by sandbags at New Cross: serving as an improvised Air Raid shelter. In the Autumn of 1941 two 4-4-2Ts were also loaned to the GWR working passenger trains in the Gloucester / Worcester area.

Jeremy Cobb collection

71

BAD DAYS AT NINE ELMS

In Part 1, we looked briefly at the bombing of Nine Elms on 1 October 1940.and the damage which resulted in the withdrawal of 'T14' No 458.

Mention was also made of previous raids although no dates were given. For the record, what follows is the complete log of incidents as affected the shed only. (Other nearby locations, notably Nine Elms Goods and Loco Junction were similarly affected either at the same or on separate occasions.)

10-9-1940, 11.40 pm: HE on shed, causing fire but extinguished by staff. Several locomotives damaged. (One only is referred to specifically, 'G6' No. 257 but which was repaired and returned to traffic.) No casualties. Further damage caused by exploding DAB.

14-9-1940, 9.30 am: UXB, cleared at 4.30 pm.

18-9-1940, 10.30 pm: Compressor House damaged.

Left - Nine Elms, 16 April 1941. No. 927 *'Clifton'* and No. 852 *'Sir Walter Raleigh'.* On the right is No. 2332 *'Stroudley'* and at left, 4-6-2T No. 2326.

30-9-1940, 1.55 am: Direct hit at west end of Shed by HE virtually destroying 'T14' 4-6-0 No. 458. RE Construction troops used to clear up the mess. (Lt Col. Mount's report, referred to five previous attacks on the depot in which four other engines had been damaged.)

17-11-40, 8.27 pm: HE damaged roof of Loco Shed and No. 25 road. (The accompanying photographs refer to the raid as on the 16 April but with the scenes recorded on 17 April.)

16/17-4-1941 (No times given): Nine Elms Locomotive Shed and Fitter's Shed damaged by HE. Two locos overturned.

10/11-5-41, 12.15 am: Crater in Nos. 7 and 8 Shed roads and in Foundry road. One locomotive ('T14' No 446) damaged (- but subsequently repaired) by HE and several wagons burnt. One member of staff injured extinguishing fires in Factory.

20-2-1944, 10.05 pm: HE and numerous IB fell near Shed, blocking Nos, 1, 3 and 4 roads. Coaling plant and main water tank were damaged and several locomotives derailed or damaged. Coaler back in use and Nos. 3 and 4 roads clear 11.45 am. ('K10' No. 380, 'N15' Nos. 751, 755, 775 and 776, 'N15X' No. 2238, 'S15' No. 841, 'Q1' No. C15, 'D1' No. 2289.)

15-7-1944, 3.18 pm: Flying Bomb fell in Gas Works on Up Side, damaging windows in new warehouse and locomotive shed. Fireman of freight train injured.

Bottom - The end for 'T14' 4-6-0, No. 458 at Nine Elms on 1 October 1940.

Right - Six months later in April 1941 the scene inside the 'old shed'. On the right is 'Schools' No. 927 *'Clifton'*, that to the left hardly recognisable as a locomotive, but is part of the twisted remains of 'Lord Nelson' No. 852 *'Sir Walter Raleigh'*. Both locomotives were repaired, No. 927 spending three months at Ashford, emerging at the start of July, resplendent in malachite green livery.

Above - Look carefully and two members of the 'N15X' class can be seen, that on the left, No. 2333 *'Remembrance'*. The other engine cannot be positively identified.

Left - Debris from the roof of the old shed litters the floor and buries the engine seen above: April 1941. Subsequent, no doubt intended to be 'temporary' repairs to the shed roof were made with asbestos sheet, although this would last until closure in 1967.

Opposite - 'Lord Nelson' No. 852, *'Sir Walter Raleigh'* minus cab, and with major damage to the firebox and rear part of the main frames. On this occasions a stick of eight bombs had hit the shed, killing two men and injuring eleven others. One bomb struck the cab of No. 852 causing the damage seen.

Left - The nameplate from No. 927 lies close to its damaged neighbour, No 852 in Nine Elms shed.

Above - According to Bradley, the damage to *'Sir Walter Raleigh'* was such that rebuilding was not considered viable and it was very likely the engine would be scrapped. A reprieve came due to continuing teething troubles with the new 'Merchant Navy' class and consequently No. 852 was disassembled and the various parts transported to Eastleigh where the frames were seen outside the works. Aside from the a new section of frames at the rear, a new firebox, cab, centre coupled wheels and axle, rear axle and tender tank were all required. On paper at least the cost of repairs was £5,794, although this was punitive compared with the £23,840 for the then cost of a new 'Merchant Navy', the latter also excluding design and other costs.

In all 189 Southern locomotives were damaged by enemy action, but it was only No. 458 that was written off. Most of the main depots also received attention from the enemy at some stage, the most seriously hit being Bricklayers Arms, Stewarts Lane, New Cross Gate, Nine Elms and Fratton. Five shedmasters received the British Empire Medal.

Not surprisingly with the degree of enemy bombing in the area, much of the immediate surrounding was destroyed. This moving account of the remains comes from Darwin, "Yet perhaps the most convincing evidence of what Nine Elms suffered is in its immediate surroundings. The visitor gazing over the wall which bounds it on the further side looks on nothing but empty gaping houses. If in all that forlorn view if there is a single window to be seen I did not see it. It looks like a little city of the dead".

One of the locomotives damaged in consequence of the 20 February 1944. The crater made by the explosion is apparent and filled by what was no doubt a ruptured water main. In steam but with its tender derailed, is No. 2328 *'Hackworth'*. (See details of this raid on page 74.)   Photos in this section from the Jeremy Cobb collection

DEEPDENE AND THE SOUTHERN WARTIME CONTROL

In the period immediately prior to 1939, the Southern was looking around for an emergency headquarters away from what was expected to be an immediate air attack on London. It was Bulleid who found the ideal location, a former hotel at Deepdene, near Dorking, close to where Bulleid himself resided. The property was already on the market for £17,000 and Bulleid offered to purchase it himself - that is before anyone was able to gain an idea for its future potential use. Bulleid's biographer, Sean Day-Lewis recounts what happened next, "Such unofficial action was frowned upon at Waterloo and Deepdene was bought through official channels for £25,000." The property had the advantage that aside from adequate office accommodation, there were a number of caves in the nearby hillside, these dating back at least 300 years, which were quickly turned into the main emergency control room. A second property at Elmstead Woods in Kent was similarly used, as was part of the Brighton Works complex.

The caves afforded a relatively safe space for the night control staff of the Operating, CME, Motive Power and Electrical Engineer's departments, various rooms connected via a series of tunnels. These rooms consisted a meeting room, 3-position switchboard, battery room, main distribution frame / maintainers room, bedroom for use of the night officer, air plant and toilet facilities. A 4 foot thick concrete roof slab provided some protection. Let into the hillside, a 60 foot vertical shaft acted as the air intake and emergency exit.

Initially Deepdene was the headquarters for most of the senior management, although the Solicitor remained steadfast at Waterloo throughout. The General Manager, after a spell at Deepdene, commuted between here and Waterloo (Missenden also lived nearby), whilst the Chief Civil Engineer and Traffic Manager were permanently country-based. The Stores Superintendent also later returned to Waterloo. Between the caves and main house, a 99 feet radio mast was erected, radio communication forming an ever increasing means of communication. (A number of mobile transmitter stations were provided in Southern territory utilising specially converted 10cwt parcel vans.)

In addition to the Waterloo headquarters, the three divisional superintendents, all formerly London based, moved their own 'battle headquarters' to specially reinforced underground chambers at Woking, Redhill and Orpington. Elsewhere the divisional headquarters at Southampton and Exeter stayed put. Due to the risk of air-raids, it became common practice for the office at Southampton to send valuable documents to the relative safety of the country at Salisbury overnight, these were then returned in the morning. Later Southampton had to make recourse to the use of a special train as a temporary mobile headquarters.

The movement of urgent paperwork between Deepdene and the various divisional headquarters was often by despatch rider or car. The SR had at Deepdene for example, some 26 cars and 14 motorcycles. The riders of the latter were themselves not always safe, as witness one, who riding without lights, found his wheels dipping into a bomb crater. Another saw tram lines blown up in front of him and was then literally blown off his motorcycle. The cars were also sometimes used to ferry a specialist to the scene of an incident or event, or even move a locomotive crew if required. Vehicles and riders / drivers were also based at the various divisional headquarters. Notwithstanding a return to peace, the switchboard at Deepdene itself was in railway use until the 1960s.

Top left - The Night Officer's room.
Bottom left - The Control room.
Right - Night Control staff.

Much further information is available at:

http://www.subbrit.org.uk/rsg/sites/d/deepdene_house/index.html

81

ENEMY ACTION

Battersea Park, purported as 15 November 1940, although it could in fact be a day later. High explosive was dropped on the local lines at 3.40 am with all lines reported as blocked. The main lines were cleared by 8.30 am and most of the other lines by 9.30 am. A full service was restored at 4.15 pm on 18 November.

Opposite page - Belmont, 11 October 1940. At 8.30 pm there was direct hit on the station house and booking office The Down platform and both lines blocked by debris. One passenger and a clerk were seriously injured. The debris was cleared by 2.55 pm on 14 October.

Above - reported as Blackfriars in 1941, but without a date. During 1941 Blackfriars was reported as having been attacked at least five times.

Blackheath, recorded as 'Enemy Action' 9 March 1945. (- possibly having occurred the day before.) The damage was caused by the nearby blast from an 'LRR' - Long Range Rocket or V2. Three electric units were affected, see page 42.

Destruction by fire of the former Cannon Street Hotel, 10/11 May 1941, previously renamed the 'City Terminus Hotel' but which closed as a hotel in 1931. After this time it became 'Southern House' being converted into office space although with large areas available to hire for public functions. The internal damage was such that it was in effect gutted. It was later necessary to rebuilt the upper two floors in plain style.

The signal is STILL
against holiday travel
THIS WHITSUN

RAILWAY EXECUTIVE COMMITTEE

SOUTHERN RAILWAY

A Passenger was

FINED

£10 & £2.2.0 costs
second conviction

on April 13th, 1944, for deliberately travelling in a 1st Class compartment with a 3rd Class ticket when there was room in a 3rd Class compartment

"**The engine that saved a bridge**. 'Schools' No. 934 *'St Lawrence'* after taking a direct hit whilst standing on the bridge outside Cannon Street, 11 May 1941. The raid commenced at 3.55 am with the terminus buildings and station roof damaged by fire. At 4.20 am a further device fell on No. 934 whilst further bombing saw penetration of the underground lines and consequently the station was closed. Three corridor sets were derailed in the west siding and an eight-car set damaged in the East siding. By 5.30 pm the same day the station was usable in part whilst the roof was still ablaze 24 hours later. All lines were open again on 17 May."

Such then is the formal account of the damage at Cannon Street that night, although it better recounted still by Darwin, "The night of 10/11 May is another of *the dates,* and this time Cannon Street shall come first with its story of men huddled all night on the bridge, not merely with bombs falling all round them but with the lively expectation of themselves falling into the river. About 11 o'clock bombs and incendiaries began to drop in showers, and the foreman and a lineman went out into the thick of them to put out fires on the bridge. When they came back they found that two heavy H.E. bombs had fallen by the side of one of the platforms; the station hotel was on fire - it was ultimately gutted - and so was the station roof. As pieces from the blazing roof were falling everywhere it was decided that the safest place for the trains standing in the station, was on the bridge, and they were moved there accordingly. The safety was emphatically relative, for the bombs were streaming down into the growing fire; some fell in the river and the splash from one of them went over the signal-box. The men crouched on their engines or took the best available shelter in the tower on the bridge, making periodical dashes out of it to try to put out a fire in the van of one of the trains. After a while even the tower failed, owing to pieces of masonry falling inside it. There was nothing for it but the naked bridge from which the view became ever more tremendous with the wharves and warehouses by the station making one long line of fire beside the water's edge, while the fumes were so thick that it was hard to breathe. As one of the firemen wrote in his report, 'It was all rather terrifying being on the bridge with nowhere to go, just waiting for daylight.' I should rather think it must have been.

"One of these accounts is so admirable a piece of description in its vividness and its modesty, that it would be an impertinence to paraphrase a word. So here it is exactly as it was taken down: - "*Experiences of Driver L. Stainer, Bricklayers' Arms.* - I booked on duty at 11.5 p.m. and left the Loco Depot at 11.30 p.m. to work the 12.53 a.m. Cannon Street to Dartford. On going up to Cannon Street between Surrey Canal Junction and London Bridge, a fire had started over by Surrey Docks and loads of incendiaries were dropped all the way to London Bridge and the City. We stopped the engine at Borough Market and the Fireman put out incendiaries. On arriving at Cannon Street, Platform 6, bombs began to drop, then the aspect signal lights all went out, and then some bombs dropped outside the station, bringing clouds of dust. A fire had then started at the side of the station, and it then rained bombs and there seemed to be no stopping. The fires were then like huge torches and there were thousands of sparks. The smoke from the fires blacked out the moon, and fires seemed to be everywhere, and then the station roof caught alight. To save the trains catching fire, two engines, coupled together, No. 934 and 1541, pulled out of Platform 8 on to the bridge. We stopped twenty yards ahead of the other train, and then, after about ten minutes we ducked down on the footplate. We counted three bombs, the last one was terrific, and very close. There was a terrific explosion and our engine seemed to roll; at first we thought our train had been hit. The debris flew in all directions - we were very lucky. My fireman said at the time, "Look out - we are going in the drink", and I said "I thought my back

week had come." We looked round, and found that the bomb had made a direct hit on the boiler of No. 934 engine, and it had also blasted our train, and turned part of the train over on its side. My fireman and myself went to see where the driver and fireman were, and I am pleased to say they had got off the engine in time. Then, looking round, we found our train had caught fire, and the fireman with buckets of water tried to put same out, but it was impossible as a strong wind was blowing up the Thames, and the fire got the master. " I uncoupled my engine from the train, and drew back about two yards, and secured the engine, and then crossed to the west of the bridge until dawn - watching the fires. It was just like as if Hell had been let loose. I am pleased to say there was no one injured and we were all lucky to be alive. Every railwayman at Cannon Street was very cool and calm, and all assisted in every possible way under those trying and unique conditions. That is my account of the Blitz."

The driver and fireman of No. 934 had escaped death by a bare minute. They had got out of the engine one on each side, and were finding their way back to the station by the side of the train when the bomb fell and each shouted to know if the other was all right.

With grateful thanks to Peter Bailey and 'The Life and Times of St. Lawrence 934 Part One' by John Richards.

Brighton, 18 May 1942. Several bombs have fallen in the vicinity of the station and what was the south west and north east corners of the works complex. As with the later 1943 raid, it appeared the enemy were attempting to focus their attention on the railway infrastructure but its close proximity to residential accommodation meant there were bound to be civilian casualties. Targeting was also not always exact and consequently bombs aimed at the railway often fell wide of the mark with devastating consequences.

During WW2, there were 198 deaths in Brighton directly attributable to air raids whilst 357 were seriously injured and a further 433 suffered slight injuries.

With the twelfth century Cathedral as backdrop, this was the scene in Canterbury Goods Yard following the overnight raid of 31 May / 1 June 1942. Hardly a strategic military target, Canterbury was specifically attacked by the enemy in retaliation for the Allied raid on Cologne. The enemy attacks were known as 'Baedeker raids', after the German issuer of an English Travel guide: it was from this guide that the Germans chose their non-military targets. 43 were killed and 81 injured here overnight. Other raids, followed on 3 and 7 June. From a railway perspective, most of the damage appears to have been concentrated on the goods yard, the area of which was also one of several coal concentration grounds, ensuring emergency supplies were distributed in areas considered to be less likely targets. At least one horse on railway property was also killed.

Signal boxes were difficult if not impossible to totally
protect, although the Southern did provide a number with
a brick outer jacket in an attempt to afford some degree
of blast proofing. Elsewhere, as at Clapham Junction for
example, a new roof was provided, whilst metal sheeting
over windows was also commonplace. None of these
would have provided much protection from a direct or
close hit, such as here at Chiswick at 10 20 pm on the
night of 20 February 1944. The main casualties were
reported as the station buildings and signal box, although
a number of properties in the nearly residential roads had
roofs and windows blown away. At this stage all lines
were closed, but were reopened to traffic at 8.00 am on
23 February, by which time the signalling had also been
repaired, albeit temporarily. (A permanent new signal
box was opened here on 11 June 1944). Even so there
were still three UXBs to be dealt with and consequently
full working was not restored until 7 March. Combined
disruption at Whitton and Chiswick entailed diverting
Reading trains via Chertsey. Windsor services were ter-
minated at Hounslow. Buses to Twickenham; with special buses also covering the interrupted service on the
Hounslow Loop. The fate of the signalman was not reported.

93

Another signal box severely damaged, in a raid on 27 June 1944, was that at Deptford Lift Bridge on the Deptford Wharf branch, at the point where the railway passed over the Surrey Canal. The incident was caused by a flying bomb which landed nearby causing structural damage with all telecommunications cut. The signalman was fortunate to escape suffering from just shock. The lady present will be noted. The box was repaired and remained in use until 10 December 1967.

At Chelsfield, south of Orpington, at 7.25 pm on 4 November 1940, a bomb struck the footbridge at the station which then fell across the 6.00 pm Cannon Street to Sevenoaks EMU service. Two vehicles were damaged and one passenger killed. There was also damage to the nearby sub-station and the up platform. The site was cleared and services resumed at mid-day on 7 November.

The results of shellfire to reach Dover from enemy positions near Calais, 12 September 1944. Seen is the damage to the 1932 built station at Dover Priory

Enemy action where a device has hit earthworks was sometimes more difficult to attend to: at least a locomotive that took a hit could be moved usually leaving the railway intact. In the top view the scene is at Gomshall and Shere on 11 August 1942, but without further explanation. (Possibly soldiers or Home Guard practising rock climbing as they are carrying slung rifles.) In the lower view the location is Midhurst on 6 November 1940, a device seeming to have struck the embankment requiring repairs to a culvert and leaving the rails and a restricted number of sleepers dangling in mid air.

Templecombe on 5 September 1942. (As commented upon in the first book, the dates may well refer to when the view was taken rather the date of the bombing. Just two days earlier, the GWR route at Castle Cary, ten miles north had been hit, the latter reported as the responsibility of a lost enemy pilot who had been seeking Bristol.) It was a rude awakening at Templecombe, deliberately targeted it was said, due to its important marshalling yards, the interchange point between the S & D and south western main line. 13 people were killed, 5 of whom were railwaymen.

SHALFORD AND GOMSHALL

The incident at Shalford in the early hours of 11 January 1944 was certainly not due to enemy action, although at least one of the trains involved contained aviation fuel en-route to Wye in Kent.

Around 3.20 am a train of 25 tank cars (plus no doubt brake van and barrier vehicles although these are not mentioned), collided with a stationary goods train near the road overbridge at the entrance to Shalford station. By implication, it may appear as if the driver of this train was at fault, although it must be said located accounts do not afford sufficient detail to reach a conclusion, neither has the Inspecting Officer's report been located.

Several vehicles were derailed and consequently damaged, so allowing fuel to escape which quickly caught fire. (there were no doubt any number of ignition sources to the vapour.) The initial blaze was confined to the first four wagons, but leaking petrol ran into a culvert and thence into a nearby stream from which vapour seeped out of the ground at several points causing a number of separate explosions.

By the time fire crews from both Guildford and Chilworth reached the scene, the flames were reaching some 50 feet in to the air and there were fears the heat might ignite a separate 60,000 gallon petrol store in the station yard. The fire crews were also hampered by initially only having water at their disposal, foam arrived later, consequently at first they were only able to try and prevent the situation worsening. To this end other tanks were cooled and sandbags placed to try and prevent more of the leaking fuel reaching the water courses.

Such was the ferocity of the flames, that trees adjacent to the line were torched as were several telegraph poles, whilst one of the piers of the road bridge was also fractured by the heat. Even so it was reported that in just one hour the flames were brought under control and were completely extinguished half an hour later. (These times must be doubtful: witness the accompanying photograph, obviously taken in daylight and still with an inferno raging.) Adjacent to the line, a local potato and vegetable merchant, Ted Gittings, had much damage caused to his stores, stock and offices. When subsequently interviewed he appeared not unduly perturbed, stating he was insured. Two men also had a lucky escape when they felt the road over bridge moving under them although one escaped without his boots, which were stuck in melting tar.

The driver of one of the trains, Arthur Griffin, was subsequently awarded the BEM for uncoupling the burning tanks and moving the front part of the train to safety. Several members of the Fire Service was also awarded honours. Both lines were reported as re-opened at 8.20 am on 11 April.

Less than two months later, another incident occurred on the same line, this time on 3 June, when Driver Thomas Tichener of Redhill, noticed two wagons of his 45 wagon train were on fire near Gomshall. One of these contained salvaged cardboard but the other was full of ammunition. Driver Tichener stopped the train and the two wagons were separated from the rest of the train which was then pulled to safety. By this time the fire was such that ammunition was exploding and cases of live shells were being flung a distance of 200 yards.

The fire brigade attended and managed to first cool and then douse the wagons using sleepers for protection and a lineside hut as a makeshift shelter. With the fire out, army teams eventually salvaged some 40 cases of ammunition.

(With grateful thanks to Frank Phillipson, Ron Shettle and 'Guildford the War Years' published by Breedon Books.)

Fire brigade vehicles outside Shalford station. Out of sight on the forecourt was an NFS Mobile Canteen, converted from a peacetime Rolls-Royce private car. In order to pump any remaining fuel from the damaged tankers into replacement vehicles, modifications were made to a portable Dennis trailer-pump by a local Fire Brigade Officer. The premises of potato and vegetable merchant, Ted Gittings, can be seen alongside the station.

JUNCTION 'X'
A BBC radio broadcast of 1944

Alastair Wilson

*I*n early1944, the BBC broadcast a one-hour programme on the Home Service (the precursor, one might say, of today's Radio 4) entitled 'Junction X', written and produced by Cecil McGivern (1907-1963). (His name probably stirs memories in those of you who are over 70.) In June 1944 the script was published in softback form (my copy, bought in early 1945, was from a second edition).

The title page explains what the programme was, and why it was written, in the following words: "A dramatisation of events that occurred at a vital crossroads on the road to victory on a certain day in 1944 between the hours of 10 a.m. and 10 p.m." and "A broadcast showing how British Railways are successfully carrying out their vital and gigantic war task in conditions of unparalleled difficulty." It also says that it was made "with the full co-operation of the L.M.S., L.N.E., G.W., and Southern Railways".

There is a foreword by the Minister of War Transport, Lord Leathers, and a preface by the author and producer, which is worth reproducing. On the opposite page is a photograph of a driver and fireman in the cab of an unknown 'Schools' class locomotive, overprinted at the bottom with "The author dedicates this book to the Railwaymen of Great Britain – Front Line Fighters."

"I cannot remember ever wanting to be an engine driver. I cannot remember ever being interested in engines. . . . engines and trains and drivers and firemen had no interest for me at all. I wasn't mechanically minded – the insides of engines bored me. Whenever I went on a train journey, I fell asleep. Altogether I grew up in shocking ignorance of railways and the stock that ran on them.

"Which," I said to myself in February, "is the reason I've been given the job of writing and producing a sixty minutes feature broadcast on railways." It takes a lot of words to fill sixty minutes, and a large amount of information can be packed into that time – must be, if the programme is to be interesting and useful. And I was rather appalled. However, a radio feature producer becomes used to turning himself into an expert on any given subject in two or three weeks. That's all the time I had, so I packed my bags and set out to explore darkest railwayland. . . . .

For the next sixteen days my life became a mix-up of railway-lines, footplates, guards' vans, docks, floating cranes, refrigerating plant, sidings, offices, marshalling yards, loco-sheds and steadily increasing gloom. Very early on in my wanderings I said to myself, "Railways are complicated things." And very soon the word "complicated" seldom left my lips. Complicated – complicated – how can I get all this on paper? Standing on the back of a freight train, in a rattling, jerking, open inspector's van, I listened (my face, I hope, showing intelligent interest, my heart, I fear, sinking into a blacker depression) to a quick-thinking, fluent-speaking railway inspector telling me about the track, the permanent way. There was more first-class programme material in one mile of track than I could get into half a dozen feature programmes. One mile of track . . . and I had to cover all the British railways . . .

At the end of my "field-work" I had a very dirty suit, with several holes burnt in it, a dirtier overcoat, with holes in it, an oily hat, oilier gloves, worn-down shoes, and in my head an uneasy mass of information. But – among other places – I had been to Crewe! [I know this is *Southern Way*, but railways are railways, and you will see the relevance in due time!] . . . The Divisional Superintendent skilfully guided my thoughts out of chaos and told me very funny railway stories with the wit and poise of a skilled raconteur. The mass of facts in my head began to click into position – one or two, here and there. I began to think of pen and paper. I left Crewe – blessing it.

I reached my desk with two main and very vivid impressions. First, the complications – surprising and extremely interesting – of railway working. Second, a sincere admiration and respect for the way the British railways are tackling the gigantic task which has been given to them. Eventually, "Junction X" was written – a sketch only of the work done at the real "Junction X," a hint only of the work if the railways as a whole. . . ."

The drama (and it is drama) had eighteen speakers (a cast list is at the end). The link throughout is through a Narrator and The Listener. Here follows some of the script, with particular emphasis of a section of 'flashback' to the railways' part in the Dunkirk evacuation of 1940, in particular, the Southern's. The remainder is not specifically Southern, but an amalgam of all the Big Four companies.

NARRATOR [*simply and sincerely*]: I should like all of you listening now to close your eyes, and in imagination to look for a few moments over the darkened surface of these Islands –

THE LISTENER [*angrily interrupting*]: Oh, for God's sake, man!

NARRATOR [*gently*]: Sir?

THE LISTENER: Yes. Your silly play-acting! Close your eyes! In imagination! There's a blitz on down here. And my imagination's travelling in only one direction.

NARRATOR: I sympathise with you – I'm sorry if I irri-

JUNCTION 'X'

Towards 'D-Day' a temporary rail connection was provided just east of the Royal Pier, Southampton, where loading facilities allowed rail wagons to be taken on and off ships.　　　　*Howard Butler collection*

tated you. . . . There's a blitz on, is there? What can you hear?

THE LISTENER [*tensely*]: Guns – bombs – aircraft – fire-engines ambulance-bells – a corner of hell.

(*The music has gone. In its place is the frightening din of an air-raid. The Narrator and the Listener listen to it for a moment.*)

NARRATOR: Yes, I sympathise. . . . Can you hear anything else?

THE LISTENER: Isn't that enough?

NARRATOR: There *is* something else. Let's take away some of the noise – take away the bombs and the aircraft –

(*They are taken away.*)

Hear anything else now? . . . Then cut out the explosions and the bells and the crash of buildings.

(*Only the sound of gunfire is left, splitting the air with noise. Then – suddenly – between two salvoes, is hear the distant familiar whistle of a shunting engine*)

THE LISTENER: (*softly*): A railway engine. . . .

NARRATOR: A railway engine. Concentrate on it. Forget the rest. . . .

(*The blitz noises are gone. The Listener hears only the distant, perky toot-toot – and after a moment the clank-clank of shunted wagons. It is held for a few moments as a soft background.*)

NARRATOR: A shunting-engine. Clanking trucks. . . .

Comforting in a blitz, isn't it?

THE LISTENER (*slowly*): Yes . . . it is.

NARRATOR: *They* won't stop because of a blitz. Unless a bomb hits them. And then others will take their place. . . .

(*Again, for a moment, only the musical clank-clank-clank of the buffers is heard. It fades to silence.*)

That noise hasn't stopped for nearly five years . . . not for one minute . . .it mustn't, you see . . . Well, it's eased your nerves, hasn't it? Brought back a feeling of normality. Can you keep the blitz in the back of your minds? And join the rest of us in our – play-acting?

THE LISTENER (*rather grudgingly*): I'll try.

(*The music begins again – low, quiet, peaceful – painting in softly the night scene.*)

NARRATOR: Darkness over Britain . . . But things to be seen in that darkness if you look widely and carefully enough. . . . The glint of rails – dull silver. . . . Hanging in the sky, coloured lights – the red and green and yellow of signals. . . . A sudden gush of ash from an engine smoke-stack. . . . a melting feather of pink tinged smoke . . . the soft pools of light from the tall light standards of a marshalling yard . . . a pin-point of light, now red, now green, swinging in the hand of an invisible shunter . . . the sudden, startling flash from an electric train . . . the small jets of light as doors are opened and quickly shut, doors of signal boxes, of warehouses, of yardmen's huts . . .

Exactly when the facility was provided is not certain although it was certainly active in 1944. (In Bert Moody's book 'Southampton's Railways'. there is an August 1944 image of a WD 'Dean Goods' shunting vehicles in the same location.) The vessels seen here are believed to be American in origin, some idea of the scale achieved from the men seen in each of the illustrations.

Howard Butler collection

tiny hints in coloured lights of the vast network that covers these Islands . . . tiny hints of immense, unceasing labour. . . .

(The music changes, ascending, as if lifting part of the darkness. There is a hint of a recurring rhythm in it. Night is giving place to dawn.)

Dawn . . . The points and flashes of coloured lights are vanishing . . . and out of the shadows emerge movements and solid shapes. . . . The dim outlines of passenger trains, moving from station to station. . . . Fast expresses, hurtling over the length and breadth of the land. . . . but there are squatter shapes, of slower movement . . . freight trains, line after line of them . . . no section empty of them . . . often no space between them . . . engine to guard's van, head to tail, four, five, six in a long slowly moving column . . .waggons – in hundreds, in blocks , , , surging slowly on . . .stopping only when no room can be found for them, when sections are blocked and relief for them is for a time impossible to devise . . . wagons . . . one million of them loaded every week . . .filling marshalling yards – waiting for space on already congested lines – spilling on to passenger lines – pouring loaded into docks – pouring loaded out of docks, running alongside ships, alongside factories, sheets pulled taut over guns and tanks, bombs and shells, over boots, machinery, food . . . wagons whose loads cannot be sheeted – tractors, landing barges, lorries, crated aircraft . . . wagons carrying closely guarded secrets.

Looking our from the hold towards Southampton itself. The obvious difficulty was allowing for variations in loading height associated with the rise and fall of the tide - however, an ingenious solution was established as seen on the next page.

Howard Butler collection

And snaking in and out of them and alongside them, the priority specials, the troop trains. . . . And watching them, and tending them, many thousands of men and women, whose lips continuously mouth three words – "Keep them moving." . . . Keep them moving. . . . *There is the problem, the never-ceasing headache.*
(*The music again changes – becoming brisker, more rhythmic. Over it the voice of the Narrator is louder and quicker. The quiet mood of the night has disappeared.*)
Full light now. . . . The movement becomes clearer, less haphazard. It concentrates round key points. . . . Each key point like a spider at the centre of an enormous complicate web. . . . And below us is one of those points, where trains and trucks are thicker in numbers, where the lines fan out into a wider stretch, a crazy criss-cross, where signal lamps hang in bewildering groups, where there are workshops, and shed and workers, platforms and porters, trains and travellers. . . . This is Junction X.
(*The music ends, leaving the mixed din of a busy main-line station – the blowing of whistles, the hissing of steam, the rattle of barrows, instructions from a loudspeaker, the banging of doors.*)
     - *You hear The Listener and a friend complaining about their train being late again and then The Narrator takes the Listener up an unnoticed staircase to the offices of the Divisional Superintendent and as they go he explains:*
NARRATOR: You see, he railway system on which you travel is a little too big to be run easily from one central office. So it's carved up into divisions. Junction X is a divisional headquarters. And every morning, at 10 o'clock sharp, a phone rings in the Divisional Superintendent's office. And he picks up the phone. At that moment all the other divisional superintendents pick up their phones. And they hold a conference with their Chief at Headquarters near London. Every morning they do that – after coming in at 8.30 and studying very carefully papers which have been prepared for them during the night. Every morning – Sundays as well – since September 3rd, 1939.
THE LISTENER: And as the result, every morning my train's late.
NARRATOR: As one of the results, every morning your train comes in. And that, believe me is something.. With luck, we'll hear a bit of the conference. Come in – quietly.
     (*The door is opened and shut gently*)
BOYLE: [*he is in London, so his voice comes to us thin and crackling through the phone*] : Well, do your best, Mr. Foster, and – keep them moving. Now, Mr. Fairbank?
DIVISIONAL SUPERINTENDENT [*He is with us in the room*]: Yes, Mr. Boyle.
BOYLE: What's your position upline?
DIV. SUP. Still bad, Sir. 12,642 upline wagons waiting to be cleared.
BOYLE: Worse than yesterday . . H'm . . What's your line position?
DIV. SUP. Heavy. Fifty upline trains alive.
BOYLE: Moving freely?
DIV. SUP. Rather slow at Stanley Junction [All the names were supposed to be fictitious, but certainly the

To reduce the chance of buffer-lock, large metal plates were hung over the actual buffers so allowing for a greater contact area. These were usually, but not always, removed when the rail vehicles were secured on-board.

Howard Butler collection

junction NE of Perth was not meant.] The position, in fact, is rather desperate all round. All the yards are heavy. We're waiting for engines at five depots. There's bound to be some late starts – likely to lead to more bunching on certain lines. I'm short of 15 drivers and firemen and 12 guards from one depot alone – reported sick. The labour problem's acute, sir.

- And so the meeting goes on. In particular Mr. Fairbank's division is preparing to receive a convoy bringing in 4,000 men and their stores early tomorrow morning. All the plans are in place, but the next thing is that the next thing that happens is that Mr. Boyle rings to say he's just been told that the convoy has been diverted from Northbay to Southbay, fifty miles nearer to Junction X, and everything has to be advanced by eight hours.

NARRATOR: [*quietly, close*] Have you ever as a small boy, Mr. Listener, dropped a pebble in a pond and watched the ripples? Of course you have. Now take a large pond, and get four small boys to drop a pebble into the four quarters of it at the same time. The ripples spread – and get in an awful tangle. Now do that again – but this time, just as the poor little ripples are about to get in an awful mix-up, drop a bigger pebble right in the middle and start some more and bigger ripples. Well, this division's the big pond – and there are a lot more than four pebbles dropped in it already. And this convoy diversion's the big pebble in the middle. But – and here's the point, Mr. Listener – *you've got to stop all those ripples from biffing into one another . . . .* Nice little problem, isn't it?

- The listener is taken two doors along to the Control Office, where his impression is of "telephones and maps", and he sees for himself the problems that this convoy diversion has caused.

NARRATOR: Is the picture clear? Six empty passenger trains and one hundred empty wagons to be transferred from Northbay to Southbay. A fifty-mile road to be made clear for them. Trains to be held up – others to be cancelled. Four empty troop trains and two hundred wagons now headed for Northbay to be diverted to Southbay. Roads to be made for them. Trains to be held up. Others to be cancelled. . . . . Tonight, 10 troop trains and 10 freight trains to leave Southbay on their long journey south-east – eight hours earlier than was expected. A road to be made for them. More trains to be held up. More to be cancelled. . . . A big series of movements suddenly flung on to a network of lines already groaning under such a strain that 12,642 waggons on it are already jammed tight - as series of movements that will affect every Division, that will affect passengers standing on small platforms more than a hundred miles away. . . . The eyes in the Control Officer never leave the maps. The phones are never silent. The ripples are spreading. Not like those in a pond – but spreading at 30-40-50-60 miles an hour.

- And so it goes on. The Listener hears some of the phone calls, and is taken to Southbay to see the Docks Manager handling the arrival of the convoy, and the first of the troop specials away – on time. He hears the complications of clearing the route for them – which affects another freight due for an outward-bound convoy which must sail tomorrow.

Back at Junction X, the Narrator takes the Listener up to the bridge, and tells him

NARRATOR: Lean against the rails and look down. . . . It's your turn to talk. . . . What do you see?

THE LISTENER: The main lines passing under this bridge, gleaming. . . . Pools of light on the platforms, split by shadows. . . . Wisps of steam dissolving under the roof above us. . . . Mail bags – half in shadow, half in light. . . . Sacks and stacks and barrows of goods. . . . And people. . . . the platforms black with their numbers. . . . A group of sailors, laughing, their head thrown back, pale yellow under the lamps. . . . Soldiers everywhere . . . quiet, stolid, British soldiers . . . and airmen . . . and silent civilians . . . the spurt of matches . . . the thin wisps of cigarette smoke . . . and women clinging to the arms of men . . .

- [As a 21ˢᵗ century aside, I do not remember so much light being allowed on the stations that I knew – but I never knew a large station, or not by night. Further on, it becomes apparent that minimum lighting was permitted on large stations until there was an air-raid warning.]

- The narrator and the Listener are joined on the bridge by the Stationmaster.

NARRATOR: Good evening, Mr. Stationmaster. We're enjoying the view of your station.

STATIONMASTER [*He speaks in a soft pleasant Welsh brogue, simply* and sincerely]: Yes, it's a good place to stand. I often come up here. I never get tired of it. . . . Fascinating to look down on them all, going God knows where. . . . [*Laughing a little*] I think you'll find a few of us roaming around here tonight. It's been a bit of a day and we won't rest till we've got it all behind us. Ah – here she is.

(*A train whistle shrieks and a freight train begins to rumble through the station.*)

Here's the special freight. Out in time, thank the Lord.

(*The train passes under the bridge with a fierce hissing of steam and rumbles on out of the station.*)

Well, if she keeps moving, that's one bit of trouble out of the way. The Control Staff will be watching her like hawks all the way up the line. . . .

(*And the rumble disappears into the distance.*)

NARRATOR: A big station, Sir.

STATIONMASTER: Aye, it gets a bit of stuff through it. It gets *the war* through it. Tell the story of this Junction and you tell the story of the war. . . . The kids first. . . . September 1ˢᵗ 1939. . . . Aye, we did a good job there, tho' I say that myself. London alone handled 1½ million people – we had to find 4,349 trains for that little lot. We had 30 to 40 trains of them through here every day. [*Laughs.*] You won't believe this little story, but it's gospel truth.

(*The general station noises have been disappearing behind the singing and shouting of children. The place is bedlam – but a cheerful one. We have slipped back to 1939, and to the evacuation of the children.*)

STATIONMASTER: Ten minutes' halt for this train, Guard?

GUARD: Yessir. Sound happy enough, anyway.

STATIONMASTER: They do that. . . . Hullo, Miss. You look worried. What's the matter? They sound fine.

HELPER [*distracted*]: It's not the older ones – it's the babies. Screaming their heads off. They're thirsty, poor mites.

STATIONMASTER: Haven't you got any milk you can give them?

HELPER: Oh, we've got milk. But they can't drink out of cups.

STATIONMASTER: Well – what you want is a few bottles.

HELPER: Bottles! Brilliant. Can we get any?

STATIONMASTER [*Now excited*]: There's a chemist just outside. [*He begins to hurry away.*] Hold the train if I'm not back in time, Guard.

HELPER [*a scream*]: Stationmaster!

STATIONMASTER: [*shouts from a distance*]: Yes?

HELPER: Don't forget the teats!!

[*The sound of the children begins to fade behind the*

Loading in process, as with the views on the preceding pages, the need to attempt to align the buffers as best as possible as vehicles were propelled on board, is obvious.   *Howard Butler collection*

general station noise and we are back in the present]

THE LISTENER: But couldn't the mothers –

STATIONMASTER: Now don't ask me, sir. All I know is that I became a wet nurse for what seemed half the babies in Britain, and in two days you couldn't find a single bottle – or a teat – in this town for love nor money. And that's my biggest memory of those days. Though we'd lots more to worry us. As those trains were going one way, others were comin' in the other – packed with men called up. And there were Ministries to evacuate and Government offices. And the freight traffic doubled and trebled. I used to come up here and wonder how in the name of God the Control Staff managed to get so many trains on the line. And there wasn't a single accident – not one child lost or injured. . . . But we had at least time to prepare for that. . . . In *one* movement we got practically no warning at all. . . .

(There is a quick swirl of music which covers the station noises and then ends full, leaving silence. . . . A telephone switchboard buzzer sounds.)

OPERATOR: Southern Railway.

WAR OFFICE [*phone voice*]: Mr. X, please.

OPERATOR: You're through.

WAR OFFICE: Is that X?

MR. X: Yes?

WAR OFFICE: Will you please be at the War Office at 2.15 this afternoon. A matter of the utmost urgency. I'll have someone to meet you in the entrance hall.

(The music swirls up again and ends. There is a knock on a door which opens.)

OFFICER: Mr. X of the Southern Railway.

WAR OFFICE: Thank you – and Phillips. We're not to be interrupted.

OFFICER: No, sir.

(The door shuts.)

WAR OFFICE: Sit down, X. . . . To start with, I must tell you that the information I'm about to give you must not in any circumstances be divulged by you to any person whatsoever. I think you will see the reason for that.

MR. X: [*wonderingly*]: Er – yes.

WAR OFFICE: This is Tuesday, May 21st, 1940 – a date, I think, which will figure largely in your memoirs if you should write them. . . . It is almost certain that within the next few days the British Expeditionary Force will be evacuated from France.

MR. X: [*after a pause; not quite taking it in.*]: You mean its going to be switched to another theatre –

WAR OFFICE: No. The B.E.F. is at this moment facing the biggest disaster in the history of the british army. . . . it will be total evacuation. We are not planning on an immediate return to the continent.

MR. X: [*beginning to see: softly*]: My God. . . . My God. . . . When? How many?

WAR OFFICE: When? – at any moment. How many? – I wish to God I knew that. I can tell you the numbers there, that is all. But your job is to plan for the maximum number.

MR. X: *Our* job?

WAR OFFICE: Yes. Not tomorrow – perhaps not the next day, but in a very few days at the most – we will

begin to extricate the B.E.F. They will, we expect, be disembarked at the following ports – Dover, Folkestone, Ramsgate, Margate, Hastings, Eastbourne, Newhaven and Brighton. We want the railways to entrain them immediately, and disperse them over the country. You understand quick entraining is essential – for all we know hell might break loose over those ports.

MR. X: What about stores – their equipment –

WAR OFFICE [*drily*]: I think, Mr. X, that you need not concern yourself with freight. We will consider ourselves fortunate to hand you over men.

MR. X: My God, this is ghastly –

WAR OFFICE: Yes, I suggest we try not to think of that side of the – er- movement. What I want you to do is this. Call – for tomorrow afternoon at this time – a meeting of the traffic managers of the other three main lines.

MR. X: May I tell them the reason?

WAR OFFICE: No. I will be there myself – and I'll give them as much information as is necessary. It is essential that this information is shared with as few people as possible.

(*The music swirls up quickly again and takes us to the next day*)

WAR OFFICE: Good afternoon, gentlemen. I'm not going to thank   you for coming. In a few days, perhaps, you will realise how necessary was your attendance –

MR. X: May I interrupt here, sir? I've thought a great deal since I saw you yesterday, and I must tell you that, in my opinion as a railwayman, it is essential for the meeting to be told the full facts if we are to do any good this afternoon.

WAR OFFICE [*after a pause*]: Very well. . . . We are about to attempt to evacuate the B.E.F. from France, to extricate them from the possibility of annihilation.

(*There is a horrified mutter of voices from the railway*

officials.)

I realise, Gentlemen, that you need time to see the full implication of this. But time, unfortunately, is short. I met X yesterday, as the Southern Railway will have the initial responsibility for the reception. X, I will be glad if you could give us your ideas.

MR. X: The B.E.F. will be disembarked at the following ports – Dover, Folkestone, Ramsgate, Margate, Hastings, Eastbourne, Newhaven, Brighton. Now will you please look at the maps in front of you. South-east of London is Greenbank. [A thin disguise for Redhill.] It is also within a short run of each of the ports named. Railway lines from Greenbank run to the ports, like the spokes of a wheel from the hub. I'm going to make it a pivotal point of the movement. As the troops are entrained, the trains will proceed immediately to Greenbank. Also, the line from Greenbank to Brunton [this was, in fact, Reading] will be closed to other traffic. At Brunton the trains can be switched to any part of the country. I feel strongly that the complete closing of the Greenbank-Brunton line is absolutely essential. Nearer the ports is Garsfield [Tonbridge]. To feed the ports with trains, I suggest Garsfield be used as a stabling ground. They will be close-marshalled there as soon as possible – head on to the ports, fully alive and complete with crews, running straight to the ports as they are needed. . . . And that brings me to the number of trains needed for the movement. It is an extremely difficult problem, as we do not know how many – er – passengers we have to handle. But I feel we must detail 150 trains for this job. I realise, gentlemen, for any one system to provide 30 or 40 or 50 trains at the present time is a big problem. But I hope you can agree and arrange for that. . . . Well, that's my plan in broad. I suggest we now discuss it and get down to detail as soon as possible.

*This and opposite page:
Safely stowed.*

Howard Butler collection

WAR OFFICE: And in your discussion, gentlemen, may I suggest that you bear in mind one aspect which may have escaped you. Your passengers will not be ordinary passengers. They will be exhausted, wounded, many of them. . . . They will be soldiers who have passed out of hell.

(*The music swells up, then gradually disappears behind the sounds of Junction X.*)

STATIONMASTER: That movement started at dawn on May 27th. It took 186 trains, not 150 – and they never stopped for nine and a half days: 323,000 men they took away from the ports. . . . And I saw drivers and firemen on trains coming into this station who were dazed with weariness. . . . It didn't make it any easier for us that the ports weren't quite the same as those planned. . . . Of course, we didn't know anything about it at first. The first train was in the station before we realised what was happening. . . . I'll never forget them – dirty, exhausted – a ghost army in a ghost train. . . .

(*A Dunkirk train clanks into the station, echoing eerily. It stops and doors bang.*)

A TOMMY [*exhausted*]: Where are we, guv'nor?

STATIONMASTER: You're in Junction X, Tommy. . . .

TOMMY [*dully*]: Junction X. . . . Junction X. . . .

STATIONMASTER: The middle of England. . . .

TOMMY [*dully*]: The middle of England . . . Christ . . . the middle of England. . . .

- After a scene of personal, human interest – a booking clerk who finds his son on one of the trains, we revert to the bridge over the station, where the Stationmaster, the Narrator and the Listener are joined by the Divisional Superintendent.

DIV. SUP. : Hello Evans. Romancing about your station, eh?

STATIONMASTER: Good evening, sir. Yes, I was looking back a bit.

DIV. SUP. : Did you tell them about the time you were running round the station with an armful of babies' bottles?

STATIONMASTER: [*laughing*]: I did. . . . You got the wanders tonight, too, sir?

DIV. SUP. : Yes. I'll not feel happy till I see the tail lights of that first special. After that it's not too bad.

NARRATOR: Is the line clear now, sir?

DIV. SUP. : Just about. It's affected nearly every train in the division since midday. Still, if that special freight can make the Linton loop before the first troop train comes through, we should be all right – provided nothing else happens – touch –

[*And he snaps off*]. The lights have gone down!

- It's an air raid, and we are next taken to a signal box, ten miles down the line, where the Narrator observes:-

NARRATOR [*quietly, close*]: Not the place to be in during a raid, Mr. Listener. . . . Lonely it feels, eerie . . . and a railway's a likely target, especially tonight. . . . But they don't look worried, do they? . . . Take a good look at them. They're the men you trust your life to every morning and every night.

THE LISTENER: [*quietly, also*]: They're – old, aren't they?

NARRATOR: They retired in 1938. They came back to help out. But don't worry – they're not *too* old. Look at their quiet faces, their steady hands. . . . There are 40 years of disciplined service behind those eyes and fingers.

- And the next event is a bomb on the line, not far from the box, where all the emergency action is taken, urgently, but unhurriedly.

NARRATOR: Lines covered with rock and soil – and fifteen miles away, racing towards it, the first of the troop specials. Come on, Mr. Listener. Ready for a footplate journey?

(*The music swells up, rhythmic and exciting. As it begins to fade, the first of the troop specials is heard approaching, rushing up to its maximum of noise. There is a scream of its whistle before the noise of the train sinks down below the music, which now acts as a background.*)

NARRATOR: The footplate of engine 1414 rocks and sways and jerks. . . . *here* is the true sensation of speed – more than in a car, more than in a plane . . the 50 miles an hour seem like one hundred and fifty . . . rock, sway, jerk . . . nothing to be seen outside . . . blackness ahead, blackness round . . . no lines to be seen . . . frightening to see no lines . . . rock, sway, jerk . . . how can it hold the lines? . . . No springs like those of a carriage to take the shock. . . . Icy air streams in past the fluttering, flapping anti-glare side curtains – air that strikes and chills back and legs , , , rock – sway – jerk . . . if only the lines were visible . . . if only there was something to be seen . . . rushing from blackness into deeper blackness . . . signals – red, yellow, and green – leap out of the darkness and whip past . . . bewildering in their speed . . . but the driver has picked out his green and his hand lies quiet on the brake. . . .

(*The music swell for a moment, then sinks again as a background.*)

The noise changes . . . on one side of the cab the gleaming wall of the tunnel seems dangerously close – the cab jerking as if to touch it . . . . Smoke billows I through the side windows . . . stinging the eyes . . . and dust fills the pores . . . out of the tunnel again . . . and the whistle screeches a greeting to an invisible signal box . . .

(*The music swells, covering the screech of the whistle and again goes to a background.*)

The fireman knocks open the round door of the firebox . . . flames lick out and the cab is filled with welcome heat and a red glow . . . lighting up the grey hair of the driver – his head half out of the window, gazing up the line, watching for the leaping signals, his hands slowly rolling a cigarette . . . lighting up the neat shoes of the fireman, shining surprisingly in this coal-dusty cab . . . lighting up the beads of sweat trickling down under the peak of his cap. . . . His shovel swings and coal tumbling down the tender chute is hurled into the red circle, turning red heat to white . . . every three minutes his shovel swings . . . 10-12-15 times in every three minutes his shovel sweeps coal into the red circle . . . then the door clangs shut and shadows fill the cab again. . . .

(*Again the music rises and fades.*)

They shout unintelligible words above the din . . . one word – or two . . . the whistle cord is pulled . . . a lever moved . . . and the air is filled with the sound of fierce hissing steam. . . . Every change of sound – every sway of the cab – is a message to them and they know to a yard at any moment exactly where the train is on the line. . . . This is indeed knowing the road. . . . The fireman seizes a hose and sprays the coal in the chute, the dusty floor and the sides of the cab – the water turning to steam as it hits

hot metal . . . he seizes a brush and brushes up slithering pieces of coal and thick dust . . . carpet brush in hand he becomes a strange housewife . . . now his face is streaked with dust and his shining shoes are covered with a dusty grey film . . . he swigs cold tea . . . and the driver slowly rolls another cigarette.

- *Back at Junction X the control team have been grappling with the problem – there is a loop line from Middleton which can be utilised – it's longer, and there will be more delays to non-essential traffic, but the troop special will be able to get through without much delay. Back now to Middleton Box.*

(*The music rises up: then begins to fade*

The troop train is heard approaching. There are four detonations and the train pulls to a standstill.)

DRIVER [*rather distant shout*]: Hullo, there! What the hell's the matter?

1st SIGNALMAN [*close shout*] Obstruction on line – bomb damage. We're putting you on to the loop as soon as it's clear.

DRIVER: Likely to be long?

1st SIGNALMAN : No – any minute. And there's no stop for you at Junction X. You've got to go straight through – to make up time.

2nd SIGNALMAN [*quiet, close*]: Loop's clear, Alec. I'll set the boards.

1st SIGNALMAN [*shout*] O.K., driver. Loop's clear. So long,

DRIVER: So long.

(*The train whistles and starts – and fades away as it gathers speed.*)

NARRATOR [*quietly*]: a little flat, isn't it, Mr. Listener? Not quit enough excitement in that, is there? Well – this isn't a thriller. Railway practice doesn't include desperate rescues in the nick of time. No signalman standing at the side of a bomb crater frantically waving a red lamp, while the train screams to a standstill, the engine's front wheels hanging over the crater edge. No – the excitement's of a different kind. Ready for the last scene? – the bridge over the main line in Junction X.

- *This drama-documentary is drawing to a close; though there will be more waiting for the ordinary passengers on the platforms at Junction X. The Divisional Superintendent, the Stationmaster, the Narrator and the Listener are joined by the Chief Controller, whom we only know as Gordon.*

DIV. SUP. Hullo, Gordon.

GORDON: Hullo, sir. Thought I'd find you up here.

DIV. SUP. How is it?

GORDON [*but weariness prevents him sounding pleased*]: All right now, sir. Up line position cleaned up. And the special freight has just reached the Linton loop. The road's clear now..

DIV. SUP. Good man . . . Gordon . . . [*and he pays the biggest possible compliment very sincerely*] . . . Gordon, you're a good railwayman.

GORDON [*moved*]: Thank you sir.

(*The station noises fill a pause*)

STATIONMASTER [*suddenly*]: She's got the road.

NARRATOR [*quietly, close*]: She's got the road. . . . Yes, there goes the signal, Mr. Listener. . . . A small disc of red light at the end of the platform turns to green. . . . That's all . . . and the hundreds of people waiting down there probably never even noticed it. . . . There goes the signal. . . . You may come through, it says to a train. . . You may come through. . . . But no hint at all of the work, the worry, the ingenuity, the complications. . . . The road is clear, it says. . . . But no sign of the effort of the many men who have cleared that road. . . Click! And red is green . . . and their signs of relief are drowned in the thunder of the wheels. . . .

GORDON: Here she comes!

(*The first troop train roars into the station and under the bridge and out of the station with a triumphant shriek of its whistle.*)

DIV. SUP. And there she goes! . . . Nice to see those tail lights, gentlemen.

(*But they make no answer as the train rackets into the distance.*)

Well, Gordon, may we go home?

GORDON: I think so, sir. You never know, of course, but I think it's safe to go to bed.

DIV. SUP. Well, I'll say good night. It's been a long day. And on tomorrow morning's. breakfast plate will be those twelve thousand wagons. . . . Happy days. . . . Good night, Gordon. Good night, Evans.

GORDON - STATIONMASTER: Good night, sir.

(*And they casually leave each other. The station noises are quieter now.*)

NARRATOR: Waggons. . . . We finish where we started. . . Can you remember the picture I painted for you? Waggons – in blocks, in hundreds, in thousands . . . no section empty of them . . . and snaking in and out of them the priority specials, the troop trains. . . . That train speeding up the line is not running only through darkness, it is running past line after line of loaded wagons . . . carrying the munitions of war for those soldiers to use. . . .

Today you watched a few ripples in one pond – one pond out of many. . . . There are hundreds of such ripples in hundreds of such ponds . . . every day, every week. . . . and it's going to get worse, Mr. Listener.

THE LISTENER: Worse?

NARRATOR: Oh yes. . . . One day there might be no trains at all for you – no milk – no morning paper. . . . If that happens, close your eyes and think of soldiers running up the beaches of occupied Europe. . . .

(*There is a fierce upward rush of music – which goes to an urgent background.*)

[*Strongly*}: Think big, Mr. Listener. Think big. Think beyond your tiny 8.30 train. Think of the convoys pouring munitions into this country. Think of the factories of Britain pouring out the weapons for our soldiers to use. Think of the soldiers pouring into this country. Think of the tens of thousands of soldiers already here – waiting, waiting for the signal. Think of the grim Nazi soldiers staring, day in, day out, across the beaches, searching the horizon beyond which lie these islands. . . *The preparation for the movement towards those beaches has already started. . . . The road is being made clear for it . . . clear for the Battle Trains of Britain. . . .*

(*The music rises, full and urgent – and rhythmic like the thunder of a train. It finishes, full, triumphant, and ends the programme.*)

The cast were, in alphabetical order:

Laidman Browne; Foster Carlin; Philip Cunningham; Roy Emerton; Freda Falconer; Cyril Gardiner; James R. Gregson; Basil Jones; Tom Jones; Duncan McIntyre; Edgar Norfolk; E.A. Naden; Molly Rankin; Ernest Sefton; Gladys Spencer; Reginald Tate; Philip Wade; Richard Williams.

The music was written and directed by George Walter.

At this distance of time, memory only records Laidman Browne (who played 'Mr. X'), Duncan McIntyre and Molly Rankin as being names one knew.

There is no doubt that this was a straight piece of propaganda, to remind those at home of what the railways were doing; and although it is fictional, it is, as will be appreciated, based firmly on fact. There are, for the purist, petty errors – the reference to tail lights in the plural, for example, and the flames licking out of the firebox door, but it is suggested that they in no way detract from the piece.

TOWARDS 'D-DAY'

Now it can be told

THIS WAS THE SOUTHERN BEFORE D DAY!

A year ago pre-D Day activity was at fever heat all over the Southern. All roads and rails led to the South Coast—to Southampton, Newhaven, Plymouth, Poole, Littlehampton and other ports. This photo., a familiar wartime scene on the S.R., shows tanks being loaded at Ashford, Kent. Two of the principal unloading stations for tanks were Winchester and Botley.

The above shows the stream of lorries, troop carriers, motor cycles and other Army vehicles arriving at Southampton Docks for shipment. Railway vehicles from D Day to the end of 1944 totalled nearly 20,000; American Army vehicles shipped (numbers still secret) if placed in a continuous line would have extended nearly 8,000 miles.

On D Day and after troops by the thousand embarked every day. From Southampton Americans alone numbered over two million. This picture shows British troops detraining at Newhaven.

Curiously despite there being a veritable plethora of material relative to the years 1940-43, 1944 and 1945 are somewhat bereft of material - so far. We must content ourselves then with the above extract from the May 1945 'Southern Railway Magazine' as well as some facts from Darwin.

'Overlord' consisted of two distinct but separate elements, 'Build-up' and then 'Follow-up'. It had taken two years to prepare for 'D-Day' with most of the effort focussed on Southampton as the embarkation point.

Consequently seen from the air, great swathes of the countryside were converted into storage depots, parts

Troops ready to en-train at Waterloo in preparation for 'D-Day'.

of the New Forest also cut away to be replaced by sidings in which were parked wagons, nose to tail. At Lockerly for example, between Romsey and Salisbury, were 15 miles of sidings and 134 sheds stretching for three miles between the trees. Some idea of the volume of traffic can be gauged from the figures for wagons dealt with at the neighbouring station of Dunbridge. In June 1938, that total was 182. In June 1944 it was 5,246: and in the complete year, 33,000. (This does not include a figure of 6,117 parcels.)

Meanwhile at Southampton Docks, work was progressing steadily on concrete cassions, 200 feet long, 56 feet wide and 60 feet high. These were built in the King George V Graving Dock, and when complete the dry dock was flooded and these vast mounts of concrete floated away to be completed - 'Mulberry Harbours'. Other massive docking components were built in similar fashion.

Meanwhile behind the scenes, skeletal timetables were being made up to assist in prioritising traffic, although certain types of invasion traffic was already being handled and indeed had been for some time. Longparish, the stub-end of the former line between Fullerton and Hurstbourne, was a munitions store, and in December 1943 received 478 wagons loads of bombs. This figure had increased to 1,431 in April 1944. Petrol was also being distributed to a number of storage sites at various stations: later to be moved again to Southampton. There was also the 72 mile pipeline from Walton-on-Thames to Lydd to be constructed, equipment for this taken to various railheads and moved to the required destination by motor lorry.

Storage space was another issue, hence new sidings were provided at Micheldever and Brockenhurst, both of which helped relieve pressure at Eastleigh. Andover Junction, Botley and Winchester were some of the main off-loading points for tanks - near the latter point, one complete carriageway of the Winchester by-pass road was taken over for the storage of military vehicles. The Station Master at Winchester declaring he never wanted to hear the word 'tank' mentioned again. In the Forest area, the

sidings at Lyndhurst Road, Beaulieu Road, Brockenhurst and Christchurch were already stocked to capacity.

Of these locations it was perhaps Micheldever that has seen the greatest transformation. From a pre-war goods service of one up and one down stopping goods working per day, at its peak it was handing 1,000 wagons daily, 24 hours a day, seven days a week. At the north end of the yard was a 2,000 feet long corrugated store spanning two tracks and known as 'Woolworths', manned by between 1,000 - 2,000 soldiers. Here almost anything mechanical could be sourced, from a nut and bolt to the complete engine for a tank: all of which stock had first arrived by rail and was similarly despatched. Most of these goods sent as 'Priority 1', certainly within 24 hours of the request being made.

Further west, the plan was for supplies also to be shipped from Plymouth. Hence stores arrived at the various south Wales and Cornish ports and were quickly whisked away to, Launceston, Tower Hill, Whitstone and Halwill.

It was alongside the Exmouth branch between Exmouth Junction and Topsham that a record was also set, one which will probably now never be beaten. In the words of Darwin: "And in this matter the West Country must surely hold the speed record for its achievement at the American Naval depot at Newcourt. It was at 12.10 pm, on Saturday 2 October that the Western Divisional Superintendent was asked by the American Authorities to meet them at 2.30 pm that day to discuss the making of a temporary siding beside the line at the point mentioned. This was so that 150 wagons of stores then on their way from the North might be unloaded. The land on which the siding was wanted was then a green field. He went to the meeting with the Divisional Engineer, who undertook to have the material to lay 1,220 feet of siding on the spot by 11.00 am 4 October. He was within an hour of keeping his word, for it was there by noon. By noon on the Tuesday American personnel had 1,000 feet of siding on the ground and the Divisional Engineer's staff had the running line connection laid in and had made the shallow embankment to carry the turn-out to the siding. Early on Wednesday morning the turn-out was joined up to the siding, and by noon wagons were in position. The Signal and Telegraph department had not been idle, having put up new telegraph poles and shifted wires. By 5.00 pm on that Wednesday afternoon the siding complete with signalling, was in use".

At Southampton Docks, there was capacity for around 3,000 wagons and plans were in place for a 50% attrition rate on the basis of anticipated air raids. Fortunately these did not occur, the air attacks that did take place now of the flying bomb type and targeted towards London and the south-east: but meaning barrage balloons and anti-aircraft equipment had to be moved to new locations at short notice.

Returning to Southampton though and the problem was now becoming one of getting empty wagons away. With only limited storage space anywhere within a large radius, trains of empties were often taken miles away. There was also the problem of timing for the arrival of supply trains. Those containing the heaviest items, tanks for example, had to arrive first so as to be loaded first at the bottom of the ships. There was just not the

space to put-off trains when they started, hence supply trains were the priority over all other traffic and then in the order they should arrive.

Further west, the American forces had taken over Poole and Hamworthy Quay for the loading of petrol. In the case of the latter, despatch riders and patrols kept the route clear and stopped all smoking, the actual service being propelled to the Quayside. Lymington also played its part ferrying naval officers from the slipway to ships moored off Spithead.

East, it was the ports of Littlehampton and Newhaven that were involved. Ammunition and more men were the main cargoes here, the former in barges.

The ships of the Southern again played their part, not as before involved in evacuation, but instead carrying men for invasion whilst others served as Hospital accommodation.

In the reverse direction, the ships were kept busy with casualty repatriation and later prisoner of war transport, prisoners being landed on Southern territory at Southampton, Gosport, Newhaven and Portland. Elsewhere Purfleet and Tilbury dealt with similar traffic.

1943 view of the SR train-ferry vessel the 'Twickenham Ferry'. For a while after Dunkirk this vessel was moored at Southampton but was later involved in transporting railway locomotives: it could carry 16 engines coaled and ready for service, and 16 wagons. It could also carry a complete Ambulance train of 14 coaches, four wagons and personnel. By November 1944 she was crossing to Calais.

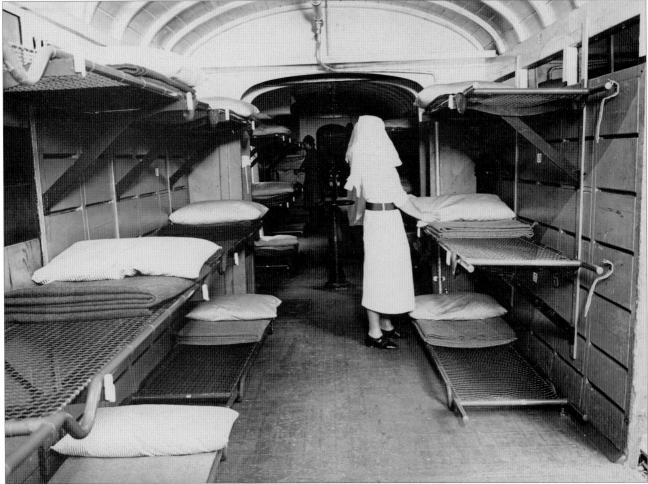

AMBULANCE TRAINS

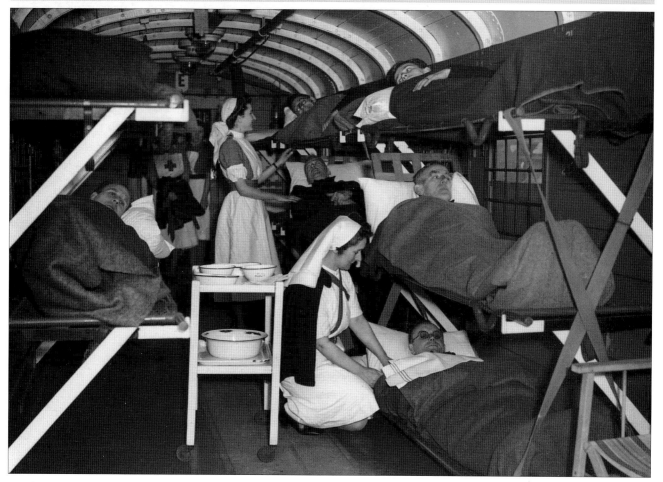

Ambulance and Casualty Evacuation trains in the period 1939 - 1945.

By May 1944 plans were in place for the movement of Ambulance and Casualty Evacuations trains from the ports to locations both on and off SR metals. (One location on the SR, Tattenham Corner is depicted overleaf.) From the SR, routes were already planned for movement on to various GWR, LMS and LNER lines.

The destination routes were as follows;

To the GWR, via: Basingstoke: Salisbury: Reading: Kensington: Winchester Chesil.

To the LMS, via: Andover thence over the GWR (former MSWJ route) to the LMS at Cheltenham (Lansdown)). Shrewsbury over the GWR from Basingstoke.

To the LNER, via: Basingstoke and Banbury.

Hospital trains were identified by the letter 'H' followed by a consecutive number. 'Home Ambulance Trains' by the identification 'HAT' and Casualty Evacuation Trains' by the letters 'CET'.

The trains ran under 'A' class headcodes with information passed in advance as to how many Cot Cases, Sitting Cases and Mental Cases were on board.

The arrival and unloading of an Ambulance train at Tattenham Corner in October 1944. The blackout precautions to the front windows of the 3SUB unit will be noted. Ambulance Train No 62 had Tattenham Corner as its allocated stabling point. Notice also the various stores in the background.

SOUTHERN WAY WARTIME SPECIAL PART 2

The image before the attention of the censor. Other than it being stated it was in the London area, no location was given although Burn Bros are known to have been makers of cast iron sanitary goods in the south London area until, it is believed, about 1959. The image was intended to show how quickly services could be restored following an air-attack in 1941. Whether the photograph was ever actually published is not reported.

Corbis Images HU033631

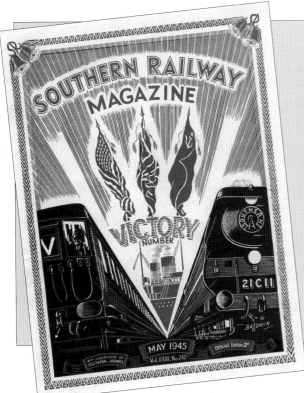

Production of a *'Part 3'* to *'Wartime Southern'* is under active consideration.

There is still a vast archive of unseen material to hand - *although more would be welcome!*

Amongst the locations we would hope to illustrate are: Crystal Palace Low Level, Forest Hill, Greenwich, Hither Green, Holborn Viaduct, London Bridge, Loughborough Junction, Hooley Cane Tunnel, Merstham, St Mary Cray, Shoreham by Sea, Snow Hill, South Croydon, Streatham Junction, Sunbury, Thornton Heath, West Croydon and West Dulwich.